Living Canoeing

L.C.1

Living
CANOEING

Alan Byde

SECOND EDITION

ADAM & CHARLES BLACK

LONDON

FIRST PUBLISHED 1969

SECOND EDITION 1972

REPRINTED WITH MINOR ADDITIONS
AND A NEW INTRODUCTION 1973
REPRINTED WITH MINOR CORRECTIONS 1975

A. AND C. BLACK LIMITED
4, 5 AND 6 SOHO SQUARE, LONDON W1V 6AD

© 1969, 1972 ALAN W. BYDE

ISBN 0 7136 1291 6   BNA -8/70 =0

Printed in Great Britain by
REDWOOD BURN LIMITED
Trowbridge & Esher

Contents

Illustrations

DRAWINGS

Foreword

Although primitive man used, and in some parts of the world people still use, canoes of reeds, wood, bark or skin, the modern sport of canoeing began only a century or so ago. Within a few years this new sport had taken root in America and several countries of Europe, and now it is an international competitive sport with a place in the programme of the Olympic Games, and has adherents in all parts of the world. This is however only a part of the picture, for canoeing is more, far more, than a competitive sport; it is a popular recreational activity akin to hill walking, rock climbing and mountaineering. Over the years the emphasis in the various branches of the sport has varied, and this has been, in part, a result of the development of new materials as well as improved facilities. During the last ten years the material trend has been towards the use of glass reinforced plastics, and this has led to the production, by amateurs and professionals alike, of cheap, durable and strong craft, highly manoeuvrable and eminently suitable for use on torrents, rough seas and surf.

During this same period there has blossomed a great development of canoeing as an adventure activity in schools and youth organisations, made possible by the growth of the National Coaching Scheme able to provide expert tuition and qualified to carry out a study in depth of old skills as well as experiment with new ones.

The author has taken canoeing as it is being practised at the present time, and has concentrated on adventure in canoeing, but he makes the point that high adventure is usually accompanied by danger, and then sets out to show what must be done to reduce this to a minimum through knowledge, good equipment, sound preparation and adequate training.

The book merits study by everyone concerned with the canoeing activities of young people, as well as by experienced canoeists. It will provide food for thought and for argument, and so will advance that steady growth in knowledge and experience necessary to any developing activity. I have great pleasure in writing this Foreword to a most valuable contribution to the literature of canoeing.

John Dudderidge, *President*
The British Canoe Union

March, 1969.

Introduction to the First Edition

My bookshelves contain about thirty books on canoeing. Most of them are about where to canoe, how to canoe and reminiscences of canoeing in years gone by.

However, none of them tells the reader how to build a glass-reinforced plastic canoe, how to build a canoe trailer, or what it is like to cope with a canoe hurtling shorewards on the crest of a twenty-ton wedge of sea water.

I live for canoeing, and intend to continue living whilst canoeing. It is in the hope that many more people, particularly school children, will take up canoeing as a living experience, that this book is written.

Although canoeing is a fringe sport it has one of the most vigorous growth rates among outdoor sports and recreations. There are about 4,000 organised canoeists and many thousands more use canoes though not members of canoeing clubs. One of its many delights is that all kinds of people can take part—in a recent training session I had two instructors, two boys from different schools, two student teachers and a deputy headmaster—a collection of individuals of widely different ages and outlooks but all having a common interest and enjoyment in canoeing. Another advantage is that it can be carried on alone or with a group—a team may add to one's enjoyment but it is not absolutely necessary. The use of swimming baths for canoeing is becoming quite common though there are still many which are reserved exclusively for swimmers. Baths superintendents take a dim view of canoes with their sharp ends, metal-tipped paddles and the residue of mud, sand and seaweed from their use in river and sea. The sight of the caretaker advancing with gloomy face and a handful of canoe debris, which he says has ruined the filters, is enough to depress the most ardent enthusiast.

Happily, however, it is now possible to obtain a canoe designed specially for baths use. It is eight feet long with a slalom-type cockpit and is in glass reinforced plastic at a cost of £5 from one's own moulds. This boat can be kept exclusively for baths use and it has round ends which should ensure that the baths remain clean and undamaged. It reacts in a very lively manner and is very good for sharpening up reflexes and providing accurate paddling practice. It is not perfect—what canoe is?—but the cost of about £10 for providing a complete canoe with paddles compares favourably with the £20 or so required for a home-made full size canoe complete with all safety equipment.

Every year sees more and more people wishing to use much the same water. Fishermen, waterskiers, sailors—the list is extensive. Inland waters are nearly all restricted already in one way or another and there is no doubt in my mind that more and more canoeists will be compelled to seek enjoyment of their sport on the sea. I use the word 'compelled' because one must never forget that the sea can be a killer. Some advice on sea canoeing is given towards the end of the book.

Most people take up an activity because they find it satisfying and there are few things so satisfying as fear overcome. The degree of fear must not be the kind which obliterates thought—what may be called panic. One may arrive at the end of an experience and think, 'That was exciting but I hope it never happens to me again.'

Take a group of children to the zoo, and lose them, and they'll turn up somewhere sometime, most likely unharmed. Take them on the sea and lose them, and you may find yourself having to answer to the police, the parents and the coroner. It is not possible to estimate the degree of mental stress that an individual can take beforehand with any certainty so it would be dangerous to set out to find fearful conditions. It is just as dangerous to set off in the security of one's own fearless nature hardened by experience, and completely forget that a youngster may find the negotiation of each little wave an awe-inspiring challenge.

I canoe because it is my life now. I remember the first time I ever canoed—inexpensive drifting with golden sunlight in bars on the sand under the rippling water. Trite but true. Twenty years later I saw the body of a young man lifted out of the water at a landing stage. He was drowned because he tried to save another young

Llangollen, 1968. Audrey Wickham, from Sunderland, braces through a roaring slot in the rocks. Watchful apprehension is a fair description of the expression. Note wrist action. (Watch is waterproof.) Remember that the noise the water makes when in thrashing turmoil such as this is quite frightening. Audrey is tall, blonde, 105lb. soaking wet, which she often is. Three women dominate the women's slalom in Britain and Audrey is one of them.

man. This other young man had no life jacket, he didn't swim very well, his canoe was not right and he had cramp. He drowned too.

Two years earlier he had been a member of the canoe club of which I was secretary. If I had known then what I know now, he wouldn't have joined the club until I, or another responsible member, had *seen* him swim fifty yards clothed and *seen* that he always wore a lifejacket when he went afloat, so that it was his natural habit, even after he left the club.

I don't feel particularly responsible for these two drownings. I'm simply determined to avoid the situation in future. This book is one way.

Introduction to the Second Edition

The tax man accepts that I became an author in February 1968 when the first sheet of paper was put in the typewriter to start this book. On 4th September 1969 the book was released to a public which is interested in canoeing rather more now and rather less then. In that time I have heard criticism, and most of that was constructive, and much of it was friendly.

One statement I make on page 13 seems to conflict with what I state on page 233. I've looked at it and wondered whether to alter it, but I have decided to leave it and ask you to judge whether the statements are contradictory, and if they are, should they be altered? So far, they stand. Canoeing is full of apparent contradictions.

The penultimate paragraph of the introduction to the first edition has given me much cause for thought. Read that, and then read an amended paragraph which follows, and consider what influences have made the change: 'Two years earlier he had been a member of the canoe club of which I was secretary. If that were now, he would join the club, and he would receive sufficient instruction for him to know his limits, to know which life jacket to wear, and when to wear it; above all he would have every reason to swim well. Safety is a state of mind, and whilst instruction is helpful, education is certain.'

Chapter 1

Access to Water

A canoe requires an area of water and a depth of water in which to move. For a baths boat the minimum size is an area ten feet square by two feet deep, and in it a canoeist can learn most of the skills necessary to become an advanced paddler. If the water cannot be brought to the user, then the user must go to the water. Access to water is very much linked with transport of canoes which is dealt with later.

BATHS

There are two schools of thought about the better way in which to begin canoeing. One favours starting in a swimming bath because this way ensures that few natural problems are presented to the beginner from the beginning, and so a steady build up to full competence is achieved. The other, and I endorse it from my own experience, is that to begin in artificial surroundings inhibits ability to tackle open waters with confidence. If one's first experience is on the beach into the gritty surge of salt water for the first capsize a certain attitude is born, a knowledge that nothing in the future can be much worse than that! To come to the beach after careful preparation in the baths and on the river is to come to it with certain apprehensions and, perhaps, a dithering and doubt which may not be present in a complete novice.

The baths are usually heated, clean and with warm surroundings. It is easy to see what everyone in the baths is doing, and there is the comforting certain knowledge that unless the girth of the paddler is less than the diameter of the outlet pipe, loss of the student down the plug-hole is unlikely. Not everyone is convinced that canoes belong in swimming baths. Canoes can bring in mud, sand which drifts on the bottom of the baths, hunks of seaweed,

13

flakes of resin and raggy bits of canvas which obstruct the filters. Metal-bound paddle tips scrape furrows across painted bath bottoms, pointed canoe ends are reputed to crack tiles (although I've never seen it happen) and plastic lined baths may be torn by canoe or paddle tip.

One County Borough is now stocking its school and public baths with at least six baths training canoes for each one for the use of school children and the public. The canoes never leave the baths which are consequently never fouled. They are eight feet long, have round ends, are a vehicle for a slalom-type cockpit with spray deck and are ideal for teaching all the paddle skills.

There are some quite expert canoeists who have never paddled a canoe outside a swimming bath. It is quite possible that baths canoeing will come to be a sport in its own right in the same way that some people never swim outside a swimming bath. Since 1966 there has been a big development of baths boats although ideas had been tried for some years before that. Canoe Polo with baths boats is an emerging national sport.

RIVERS

There are rivers and rivers. If it is a young river, geographically, it may only be canoeable in spate, or semi-flood. Even so, it should have useful pools in it at most water levels. It will generally be shallow but with hidden 'drop-offs' into deep water, sunken tree branches to entrap the legs and clothing, untreated sewer outfalls from farms a little further up river, broken bottles from picnic sites, old cycle frames with raggy metal edges and landowners who must be approached first. There may be fishermen who are not overpleased about the interference, real or imagined, with their expensive fishing rights.

Mature rivers will probably have weirs which may be great fun or killers. There will be fouling of the river, from nearby towns, tips where loads of rubbish are dropped into the river, and so on. Really the question one should ask before using a river is, 'would I mind swimming in it?' Access to the water is usually across someone's land although people have scrambled down the side of a bridge on a rope in order to launch the canoes. Some schools have landing stages for the benefit of the rowing crews and may be willing to allow others to use their access points by arrangement. Rivers go down to the sea and become estuaries in which vast areas of mud are exposed at low tide. Swift currents run off the mud flats and may carry off a group who find themselves helpless to do anything about it. Higher up where the tidal effect is just felt steep muddy banks may be exposed at low tide. The seal launch is great fun in these conditions though getting out is not so simple. I would be reluctant to take novice groups on estuarial waters unless I knew exactly what the water would do at any given state of the tide. Access to estuaries is usually across marshes and mud flats. The few tracks will probably be across farm lands and require prior permission for use. A likely place to try is a ferry site, past or present, as there is usually a group of houses there with good road access and an Inn where warmth and a telephone may be found in an emergency.

Somewhere along the river there are likely to be large country estates completely enclosing it on both sides and teeming with game and shotguns. It is not always possible to know exactly when one glides from farm land into the confines of such an estate. One peer of the realm tackled me with some asperity . . . 'Why didn't you tell me you were coming? Eh? I could have watched you fellers shooting the rapids. Let me know next time, please do . . . 'phone the estate office, you're almost always welcome.'

CANALS

Canals range from things of beauty to stinking ditches. A rather dirty little-used canal spur which ran at the back of the school where I once taught was, I found, very useful for teaching beginners. Canals are usually long enough and rarely wider than about thirty feet. Provided that the beginners have done their swimming and capsize drills in the baths, use of the canal is great fun. I would not normally have more than eight canoes on the water at one time—more would be difficult to keep under proper supervision. It is necessary to limit the canoeing stretch and all this length must be in full view from the tow path. When supervising, I find it better to stay on the bank and so be able to run to the scene of a difficulty. Only a really serious emergency would require my presence in the water.

Permission to use canals is necessary. British Waterways Divisional Offices have varying reactions to requests for permission. An application for a licence to use the canal requires one to state the name of the boat although these days many canoes don't have names. Schools may have their own canoes but share licences through the PE Organiser's office. The whole matter is rather confused at present and one or two Authorities have referred the matter to local Sports Advisory Councils for advice and resolution. The whole matter may be resolved by the present sorting out of water usage by many sporting bodies through the Government. Voluntary registration of canoeists is under discussion.

LAKES AND PONDS

A number of Education Authorities have established outdoor activity centres on lakesides, and access may be possible through them, although they have such a heavy work load that the responsibility of having strangers using their landings may be more than they are prepared to bear. Some lakes, such as Windermere, are rights of way, but because of their popularity it has become necessary to police them with fast launches. Houses with lake frontages are very expensive and one may be denied landing there. Wind storms, as on Ullswater, may blow up with vicious speed and power. A calm lake with a gentle breeze may soon become a grey wilderness of slicing spray. Loch Eck has been seen to erupt waterspouts six and ten feet high under the screaming williwaws of wind whipping down from the crags.

Ponds may be available in farming districts, but many have the fishing rights let to angling clubs. Sewers may empty into them— one very good pool which is the property of an Education Authority cannot be used until the untreated sewage from the house is dealt with in a proper way which may cost thousands. However, sailors and canoeists can have a fine time on local brick ponds up to six acres in area. A useful way to coach young sailors on restricted waters is from a canoe as it can go upwind a lot more quickly than they can. If the wind is strong enough for them to sail away from the canoe downwind, it is too rough for youngsters to be out sailing!

THE SEA

I really do not know whether I would take beginners on the sea; so much depends on the state of the tide, tidal currents, wind direction, weather forecast, launching site, accessibility, land resources and so on. Use of the sea really does demand an intimate knowledge of the place before beginners are taken on it.

I have found with the sea that quite small difficulties become complicated by other difficulties which, if taken on their own would be of little account, but which taken together become almost insuperable and result in 'epics' as one outdoor activity centre so charmingly puts it.

BCU ACCESS ADVISORY COMMITTEE

The British Canoe Union has a committee which has river 'advisers' in various parts of the country. These advisers are skilled canoeists and know their areas very well. They know most of the difficulties that local rivers present and they know where the best sites for various uses are to be found. Some may be thirsting for grade 4 terrors; the Hell Hole, Howe's Horror, The Nunneries, Stanley Weir, Serpents Tail, Miners' Bridge, Appletreewick, Salmon Leap and so on. Others may want an improver's stretch for youngsters basically capable, but as yet unstretched, others may want a long plonk to build up stamina, like the Conway estuary, the Mawddach or the Tay.
I believe that what is required in canoeing (the advisory service to some extent provides it) is not an Advanced Kayak Certificate so much as an Advanced Certificate endorsed, say, (Tees) or (North Wales Coast) or (North Pennine East) or (Solent).
Join the BCU, and use the service, leap years ahead of the unattached canoeist and enjoy canoeing at the best places.

SPORTS ADVISORY COUNCILS

Recent developments have pointed the way to the need for some recognised and respected body which will help sporting organisations to obtain use of water sports sites inland and on estuaries. This will certainly entail restriction on use for a few, but it will ensure some use being possible for all. The CCPR report, *Inland Waters and Recreation* explains some of the problems.

THE LAW

A court case in Yorkshire in 1971 took a canoeist to court accused of interfering with fishing on a river. The judge acquitted the canoeist, but the anglers took the case to appeal, and won 50p damages. Access to rivers for canoes is still in the balance. The price of freedom is eternal vigilance.

Chapter 2

Choice of Canoe

There are many different kinds of canoe and each is suitable in its own way for one or another type of work.

Available water

If baths are handy, a canoe designed for and limited to baths use is recommended. Otherwise use a slalom canoe.

Small rivers with sharp turns and overhanging bushes require a canoe which is easy to turn—a slalom type.

An estuary calls for a sea-going canoe which does not turn easily and which is directionally stable. A mature river may require either a slalom or a sea-type canoe or, more likely, a general purpose canoe which is fairly manoeuvrable and will run in a fairly straight line. It is not a good sea canoe nor is it good at turning sharp corners without the exercise of strength and skill.

Canals are suitable for baths type boats, surprisingly enough; and for slalom and straight-running canoes. Much depends on what you wish to do on the canal.

Lakes and pools require either slalom, sea-going or general purpose canoes. Real lakes, such as Ullswater, may be suitable for eskimo kayaks but the large barge with mum, dad and the kids on board will carry so much windage as to make it dangerous in gusting winds. Slalom canoes can be a serious trial to all but the experts in side winds as they twist and turn off course most infuriatingly and produce weariness through frustration.

The sea is the place where canoes are put to the test. Surfing requires a slalom canoe or an eskimo kayak. Deep water canoes are directionally stable and may carry rudders; certainly they are stuffed with buoyancy and have deck lines which are essential and which must be properly attached and used.

Future demand

The beginner may take a canoe and use it with little thought of what other jobs it may be required to do. For example: the baths boat is fine in the baths but hopeless on the open sea and potentially dangerous on the river. It is the most wonderful, thrilling sport to ride the little beast in three-foot surf when most other paddlers are swooping over the wave crests with little thought for them. It would be next to impossible to take a beginner from the baths and develop his skills in the baths boat on sea and rivers until he could enjoy surfing of that quality.

A slalom canoe, the extreme versions of which are called slalom machines, is usually small and highly manoeuvrable. It has little space for storage of camping equipment and most of the commercial canoes have large centrally placed blocks of plastic foam which take up so much room that bulky equipment cannot be put in as well.

The slalom canoe will be fine in the baths and is great on young rivers and surf, but as a lake or sea canoe it leaves very much to be desired. It is slow over a distance because to gain ease of turning the waterline is reduced and, hence, speed through the water. It won't take much equipment either so it is not much use for camping unless backed up by vehicles.

The sea canoe is a very specialised canoe. It lies low in the water, it is fast over a distance, and would be fine on canals and lakes. It is useless in baths except as a rolling trainer and is likely to be damaged if carrying rudder equipment. In surf it runs 'big gun' fashion, straight in. The slalom canoe swings and swerves about the wave face in 'hot dog' fashion. In shallow young rivers the sea kayak is a handful for the expert.

A white-water racing canoe is first-class for going downstream quickly or out into heavy surf because it is designed to lift or cleave through heavy head waves. It is rarely useful on open water in a side wind; but one of the best canoes in side winds and one of the worst are both designated white-water racing canoes.

A Canadian canoe, propelled with the single blade is great fun on rough water and in the baths, but it is very difficult to handle on open wind-swept water. The traditional kind is good for camping purposes, carrying literally a ton of gear with two or more paddlers. The white-water and slalom Canadian canoes which are now taking hold in Britain and which were developed on the continent are possibly the most water-worthy canoes there are in rough water but techniques are quite different from traditional Canadian paddling.

There are many kinds of canoe and the racing class boats are sometimes attractive to schools. These are usually built down to a low weight and, unless especially strengthened for rolling, tend to lose their decks under the considerable strain of rolling practice. The less extreme models can be suitable for touring and, of course, as they propel easily, they are not so tiring over a distance on smooth water. However, like a sea canoe they present problems in young rivers and they are not much use in baths.

SELECTION OF CANOE. GENERAL CHARACTERISTICS

	Baths	Slalom	Sea	GP	W/W racing	Flat racing	Trad. 'Canadian'	European 'Canadian'
Baths	★	★		★				★
Young river		★		★	★			★
Mature river			★	★		★	★	
Estuary			★	★		★		
Sea			★	★				
Canal	★	★	★			★	★	
Lake		★	★	★		★	★	
Pond	★	★				★	★	★
Surf	★	★			★			
Camping			★				★	★
Beginners	★	★	★				★	
Improvers	★	★	★		★	★		★
Canoe Lifeguards		★		★				
Competitors		★			★	★		★

The star indicates what type of canoes are likely to be useful on which types of water.

HANDLING CHARACTERISTICS. GENERAL TRENDS

		Length			Bottom		Beam		Section				Gunwale			
		Under 13.6	13.6–15.0	Over 15.0	Rock-ered	Flat	Under 24 in.	Over 24 in.	Flat bottom	U	Flat V	Sharp V	High	Low	Sharp edge	Round
Stability — Directional	Low	★			★			(★)	(★)	★				(★)		
	Medium		★				★						★			
	High			(★)		(★)					★	★	★			
Stability, lateral — Initial	High							(★)	(★)	★				(★)		
	Neutral					(★)				★	★				★	(★)
	Low						★				★	★	★			
Secondary	High						★				★	★	★			
	Neutral										★		★	★		
	Low							(★)	(★)	★				(★)	★	(★)
Flip Over	Sharp											★			★	
	Gentle			(★)					(★)	★						(★)
Speed	Racing				★		★					★	★			
	Fast		★			★	★				★		★	(★)		
	Slow	★							(★)	★						
Load carrying				(★)		(★)		(★)	(★)	★			★			

DESIGN

It is possible to look at a canoe and estimate its likely performance.
A good plan is to begin the examination at the point where one
makes contact with the canoe—the cockpit.

Seat

The seat must be comfortable. One may be slotted into the canoe
for three or four hours and conditions may prevent any rafting up
for the easing of numb legs. If the shape of the seat is close to the
anatomical shape then it is likely to be good. As you sit, put your
hand under your behind and feel the hard bony structure close to
the surface. If one sits on a flat, hard surface the bones begin to
push against and compress the flesh and after a few hours a
considerable bruise develops. Necrosis of the tissues follows as is

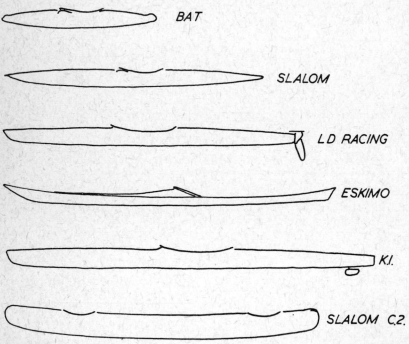

BAT

SLALOM

LD RACING

ESKIMO

KI.

SLALOM C2.

PROFILE

shown by a study of bedsores. A low seat gives stability, a high seat paddling power.

Footrest

The footrest, if wrong, may kill. It has been known for the impact of the bows on an obstacle or sea bottom when in the loop position to cause the canoeist to smash through the footrest, ending up like the ice cream in a cornet. Then again, the feet slip over the footrest and when urgent need of withdrawal is upon one, the feet are locked in and skin or life may be left behind. The footrest should be a bulkhead completely closing the front of the canoe and able to stand a 15 m.p.h. impact by a 15 stone weight. Avoidance of locked-in feet is also the reason why wearing any kind of boots is lunacy in canoes.

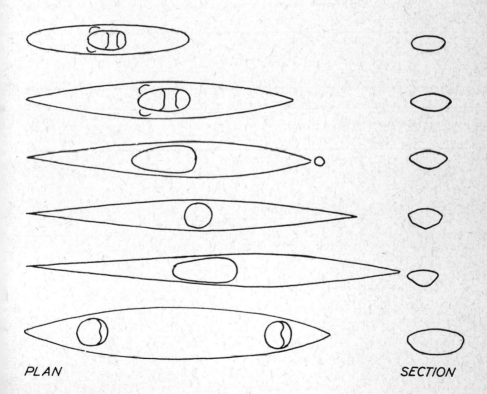

PLAN   SECTION

Knees

One must allow a place for the knees. In slalom and rough water canoes one must lock oneself into the canoe. The bottom, knees and feet make a pentagon against which one braces the reactions of the body and so generates muscular power for handling and propelling the canoe. Upside down before the roll, one is hanging from the knee braces. The weight is off the seat, the feet are pressing forward to ensure that the knees are locked into position and the reaction to the thrust of the feet is taken by the base of the spine. The knee braces must be comfortable and strong. A weight equivalent to about two thirds of the body weight is borne by them during the roll and this makes no allowance for the kick up by the lower knee necessary for the hip flick in the roll. That is why rolling a lightweight canoe built for racing is likely to end in extensive repairs.

Cockpit rim

This is usually a standard size made for people around 5 ft. 6 in. to 5 ft. 10 in. tall. Smaller people have difficulty in placing the knees in the braces, and bigger people find that the thigh length measured from the base of the spine to the knee cap is greater than the length of the cockpit opening. They must perch in unstable equilibrium on the rear deck whilst slipping their legs into the hull. If it is too wide, say more than 18 in., the water will force in the spray deck and, of course, one has difficulty in reaching the knee braces. If it is too narrow, say 14 in. or less, the hips must be twisted most painfully to wedge the backside into the cockpit. For beginners, I prefer a cockpit opening which is fairly wide, say 17 in., about 27 in. long and which is fairly square, with the width of the cockpit carried well forward to where the knees are. The front of the cockpit is round. Many of the latest canoes have egg-shaped cockpit rims which are very narrow at the knee position, the idea being that if one is good enough to go in for such a canoe, one is good enough to roll it every time. The early KW4 cockpit rim was almost ideal for easy exit.

Waterline length

The longer the canoe is at the waterline, the easier it will be to paddle in a straight line and the less easy it will be to turn. The length also adds a small component to lateral as well as longitudinal stability (looping characteristics).

The flatter the keel line, looked at from the side, the less easy will the canoe be to turn and the easier it will be to paddle in a straight line. A flat running keel is seen in a K1 and a highly rockered keel in a slalom boat. Negative rocker is usually a building fault and makes the boat difficult to turn. It has little to commend it.

The flatter the bottom, the more stable the canoe will be initially, but the flip over point will be more sudden in its onset. The more of a vee bottom the canoe has, the less stable it will be initially but the more gentle will its flip over be, and it will feel a better boat to handle after a little practice. A pronounced vee bottom makes for a racing canoe and this becomes very unstable initially causing one to lose confidence. The lack of initial stability is so great that the tip over is violent and the residual stability to be obtained from the flare out of the sides is lost in the rush.

A narrow canoe is generally less stable than a wider canoe, but the cross section shape is most important. A good shape to go for is a slalom shape—a 'U' shaped bottom with a little 'V' in it and well rounded sides with a high gunwale line. The beam should be about 24 in. and not less than 20 in. The baths boats are 20 in. wide and surprisingly stable for such a narrow beam, the secret being in the section shape.

The height of the gunwale line is most important in rolling and lateral stability; the lower it is the flatter the bottom must be, hence the initial stability is high but the flip over is sharp and the roll requires a sudden flick effort to put the hull back on even keel. A low gunwale line is where the side view shows the line of maximum width to be between 5 and 7 in. above the keel line at maximum beam. A moderate to high gunwale line will probably reduce the initial stability but the rolling characteristics and residual stability will be good.

A hull which had a maximum beam 24 in. above the keel would be difficult to tip over. It would also be difficult to see out of, still less paddle.

The plan form tells a story. If the shape is rectangular with pointed ends it tends to be a 'barge', is probably a load carrier, sits high in the water when unloaded and carries a lot of windage as a result. If the shape is diamond with a long lean entry and exit it is likely to be a fast canoe, suitable for racing or efficient propulsion over long distances. Fish form is where the maximum width is ahead of the cockpit. I find this a difficulty sometimes, to have a lot of canoe in front of me. The 'Pointer' shape, with maximum beam well behind the cockpit is common now to all kinds of canoes built for speed. Its big advantage is that the paddle can travel close to the centre line of the canoe for most of its swing.

Profile is important, especially as it concerns the deck. Rocker has already received mention; a high foredeck will probably allow it to lift through heavy waves, and make for less wet travel. Low decks will allow a slalom canoe to dodge high hanging gates and so the chances of incurring penalties will be less, but it will bury its nose in stoppers, wallowing and looping on big surf waves. A high foredeck usually implies a steeply pitched deck and with glass reinforced plastic this means a strong weight bearing section. A low deck means a low rounded deck with less vertical strength. Deep-water rescue techniques may put as much as 2 cwt. load on a foredeck. Look for a high foredeck for beginners and in sea canoes. If the rear deck is high, it is likely to be a load carrier but a high rear deck interferes with rolling ease, and a high back to the cockpit will cause bruises in the flesh just about level with the top of the pelvic girdle (like the bedsore problem). Lower rear decks than foredecks are usually a good point.

The complete canoe must have strong attachment points for deck lines. The glass reinforced plastic canoe usually has a solid resin block at each end through which a hole, either bushed or otherwise, is drilled. A strong line, preferably nylon, Ulstron or terylene between $\frac{1}{2}$ in. and $\frac{5}{8}$ in. circumference, is looped through it either as a grommet about 3 in. diameter, or as a strop knotted, re-laid or spliced. It is dangerous to have a large loop in the end strop because fingers have been severed by a rolling, waterlogged canoe in a rapid, turning and turning until the finger end is squeezed off. The purpose of the end fastening is to be an attachment for a deck line which must be reliable in use in deep water rescues and towing, and grasping in difficulties on capsize. Slippery, highly polished GRP canoes are difficult to hold. The deck line should run through deck guides level with the front of the cockpit so as to keep them out of the way, but ready for immediate use. Deck lines not so secured tend to become wrapped about the canoeist during a deep water exit or re-entry. A towing point should be fixed to the canoe immediately behind the cockpit. If towing via an end loop it becomes very difficult to turn one's own canoe, as the load is applied at the end and not the middle. Provision must be made for buoyancy in the canoe especially GRP canoes which have a specific gravity of about 1.4 and so are to be expected to sink when swamped if not supported.

MATERIALS

The canoe may be built in frames, stringers and canvas, sheets of ply stitched together and sealed, cold-moulded using strips of veneers, or a sandwich construction using thin sheets of ply re-inforced with glass cloth resined to the inside. Other methods exist, but the one which has my enthusiastic support is glass re-inforced plastic (GRP), usually known as glass-fibre. I find that once the methods·of use are known and the moulds obtained, the method is quicker, easier, less expensive and produces a more durable canoe with safety features which other canoes cannot match; for example, how does one attach a deck line to a canvas canoe so that it stays attached? GRP requires an initial outlay for the mould and some amateurs have moulds available for copying these days, although it may not be easy to find one which isn't in constant use. Material cost for building a mould is between £15 and £20 and the mould should build 20 or 30 canoes without a lot of correcting. Manufacturers expect the mould to last for 200 or 300 canoes, but their moulds weigh several hundred-weights and are made of more expensive materials. Each canoe should be built for about £10 to £12—the cost of the materials. In order to obtain materials at an economic price, one should try to buy at least £60 worth. One method is for an Education Authority to buy in bulk though this raises all kinds of other problems. A school with £60 to £70 to spend and access to a mould should be able to build their own mould and four canoes and still have something left over for future occasions.

Ply canoes may be built from kits for about £16, as can canvas canoes. Partly completed GRP canoes with canvas, ply, or GRP decks can be bought in kit form at about £25 (but better results in the long run are obtained with all-out moulding techniques from the beginning).

Completed canoes can be bought from £30 upwards. New methods are now available for vacuum forming over heated moulds of new thermoplastic materials (ABS). These are expensive in terms of machinery and moulds, but series runs of a thousand may reduce prices to half of what canoes cost now. This won't happen for some time yet, but when it does it may not be worth building in GRP because to buy a complete canoe will not cost very much more.

Chapter 3

Paddles

The paddle is more important to the paddler than the canoe. The canoe enables the paddler to stay above water most of the time, but the paddle is essential to the handling of the body-canoe-paddle unit.

The paddle has weight. One paddles by hanging this weight in front of the chest from the extended arms and then swinging it about. Paddling certainly develops the arms and shoulders and chest muscles. The perfect paddle would weigh nothing, be as springy as the best racing shafts laminated from spruce and ash and have the toughness of the best tool steel. It would cost about five bob, last for ever and out at sea it would automatically eject star shells and send out Mayday signals when the distress button was pressed!

Unfortunately, however, all paddle design is a compromise. Most novices will handle most paddles with equal ineptitude. Later skill blossoms and a certain choosiness must make itself evident as the enthusiast begins to know what is required by him. To begin with, the flat-bladed alloy-shafted plastic-sheathed paddles retailing at about one-third of the cost of custom-built paddles will be generally satisfactory, although I find them rather dead to the feel and lacking in spring and life. Therefore I have spent two or three times as much on my custom-built one-piece laminated wooden paddle.

The beginner paddles from the elbows and shoulders only. Later, he learns to bring in the power of the trunk and the thighs, and then the full drive comes all the way up from the toes braced against the footrest. There are many paddling styles and many arguments as to which is the better. The best paddling stroke is that which allows the paddler to travel from where he is to where he wishes to be in the minimum time, with the minimum effort and with the maximum of enjoyment. It must be an efficient stroke.

The effort applied to making the canoe-body-paddle unit move is generated in the human body. The principle of action and re-action shows clearly that a downward and rearward strike of the blade onto the water must be equally balanced by an upward and forward thrust of the body in the canoe. The contact between body and canoe is, as has been explained, of prime importance in canoeing. The canoe is put on like clothing—one does not climb into it.

Wide beamy barges suitable for inexpensive drifting require long paddles because many youngsters will have difficulty in finding the water with short paddles. Narrow beam canoes with what I would now call a normal width of 2 ft. require a much shorter paddle which the novice finds less difficult to handle.

Function of the paddle

The shaft of the paddle is a lever with the blade providing the fulcrum. Often in rough water handling the paddle is used as a water deflecting vane whereby chunks of water which have weight and require power to accelerate them are moved off some way by the angled blade. The reaction to this acceleration is transmitted to the arms by the paddle shaft and the arms brace, and are braced by the body, the body by the legs, the legs by the canoe sides and seat and the canoe sides by the water, making the power circuit complete. The feel of the paddle in the water is as much dictated by the hull shape as by the paddle design. The designer must consider the body-canoe-paddle assembly as a unit.

The paddle as a lever

If the paddle is thought of as a lever which is used to push the canoe past the blade, and not the converse, then it is clear that the design of the blade is important. If a fulcrum, or hingeing point is to be effective it should not slip. The paddle blade drops into a given area of water and should be withdrawn from the same area of water at the end of the stroke, without turbulence or splashing. The eskimo blade is about 2 in. wide, and 2 ft. long and the European blade is 5 or 6 in. wide and 10 or 12 in. long. Both are suited to the jobs they have to do. The shape of the eskimo paddle is dictated by the fact that the seal hunter normally paddled fifty

miles a day, swinging steadily along on flat water with no splash
from the blades. Accelerations of the body-canoe-paddle unit were
rare, as when actually killing a seal. The European blade is squat
in comparison and splashes unless handled with extra care but it is
very useful in the sudden violent surges of power necessary in
white-water rivers and on rough seas. Both are, however, used as
levers. In each case the blade is designed for the basic job as
fulcrum but is then modified to suit other requirements.

The best European blade is concave on one face and convex on the
other. The concave, or hollow face, is the drive face across which
the reaction necessary for the power of the paddling action is
derived from the water. If the water stays in close contact with the
drive face, then power is transmitted effectively. If the strike is
slow, the water slides off the face; if the strike is too swift the
water breaks down into turbulence and froth, a clear signal of
wasted energy. The hollowing of the drive face is to reduce the
rate at which water will slide away from it. Some blades are spoon-
shaped but the majority are curved in one plane only. Most of the
slalom canoeists use curved blades now. The back of the blade,
that is the convex surface, is used for backpaddling actions. The
blade should never be reversed for reversing actions—there is
never time for this in real emergencies.

Water deflecting vane

When the canoe-body-paddle unit is moving relative to the water,
instead of applying power to lever the unit in a particular direction,
one may put the blade into the water in such a way that it is held
firmly in place against the rush of the water about it, the angled
blade ploughing out a section of water and deflecting it at the same
time. Every action has an equal and opposite reaction, so a
properly handled paddle and shaft will transmit this reaction to the
body, thus causing the desired movement. Remember though, that
if the body is not fitted to the canoe it is quite possible for the
unwary to find themselves travelling quickly in the desired
direction, firmly gripping the paddle as directed but having been
unseated in the process and leaving the canoe behind.

Feather

The blades of the European paddle are at right-angles to each

Correct grasp — hand spacing.

other. This is for a number of reasons, one being the reduced wind resistance to the upper blade as it slips through the air. There is a disadvantage in that the feathered blade does catch side winds, especially at sea, leading to tipping movements unless one reacts at once to the displacing effect. Feathered flat blades may be used right- or left-handed but curved or spooned blades must be 'handed'. A right-hand blade is that which, when the paddle is held vertically in front of the body with the hollow face of the lower blade toward the toes, then the upper blade will have its hollow face turned to the right. The converse applies for left-hand blades—lower hollow facing the toes, upper hollow facing left.

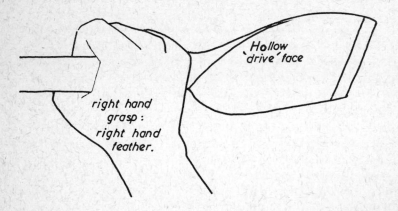

right hand grasp : right hand feather.

Hollow 'drive' face

Right hand feather

Shaft length

As explained previously, wide canoes require long paddles. A long paddle is over 8 ft., tip to tip and a short paddle as little as 6 ft. A good rule of thumb is to stand the paddle on end in front of the body, lower blade tip by the toes; check its feather and length by reaching up with one hand and resting the fingers over the upper blade tip. This should be possible without stretching for it and with the feet flat on the floor and the arm slightly flexed. Paddle shafts should be one-piece—a violent effort as when sprinting or in the rough has often resulted in the paddle coming apart at the joint in the middle where the brass ferrule plugs into the brass sleeve. This test for selecting paddles of the right length is intended for canoes about 24 in. wide. Slalom canoeists tend to use somewhat shorter paddles and sprint paddlers longer paddles than suggested. Experience will lead you to the particular paddle which satisfies your needs.

EXERCISES

Do not insist that your bunch of eager beginners spend half an hour in paddle exercises when within sight and sound of rippling waters and exciting canoes. Then is the time to let them loose within, of course, closely confined limits as unobtrusively placed as possible. The exercises come afterwards or before, but not during.

L.C.2

Ray Calverley. Note crash hat, buoyancy aid, determined expression.
Problem: Is it a right- or left-hand feathered paddle?

Arm and wrist exercise

Take the paddle in a normal grasp, arms bent, both hands at
shoulder height. Rotate the wrist backwards until the drive face of
the right blade is turned upwards and the elbow is bent upwards.

This is an extreme effort. Rotate the shaft away from the body, and the blade should turn over through 180 deg. then 360 deg. until the wrists are bent in and toward the armpits, shoulders braced forwards and the wrists feel strained. The purpose of this is to find out if anyone in the class has extreme difficulty in doing it. I haven't found one yet, but when I do, I shall know that there is some arm injury which prevents this range of movement, and I shall be able to make allowances for it right from the start. Ordinary feathering requires a 90 deg. twist of the shaft, and the exercise effectively squashes anyone who says they cannot do it because they just have.

Shoulder exercise

Take the paddle in a normal grasp. Then widen the grasp until the hands are just about touching the part where the blades join the shaft. This is not possible with long blades but one should take a very wide grasp. With paddle held horizontally across the chest swing it into the vertical position at one shoulder and press the paddle around behind the shoulder. The upper arm must now be thrust straight down until both arms are straight down at full extension behind the back. Pick up your paddle and do it again until you can hold it all the way round. The arm which was initially lower now swings upward and the paddle is brought round to the vertical position at the other shoulder, swinging it round from behind the back. Try not to duck the head. Return paddle to the rest position across the chest. Repeat a dozen times, then do it with opposite rotation about the shoulders. This is designed to show that the novice has no shoulder injury which may preclude a full movement of the shoulder muscles. It also emphasises the need for supple shoulders in the paddling effort and removes creakiness and stiffness at the beginning of a paddling session. It may be used to limber up before going into the canoe.

Trunk exercises

This can be done with about 70 lb. on a bar, but do make sure the clamps are tight and will not slip and that others are not within striking range.

Place the paddle across the back of the neck, over the shoulders; rest the arms over the top from behind so that the hands rest palm

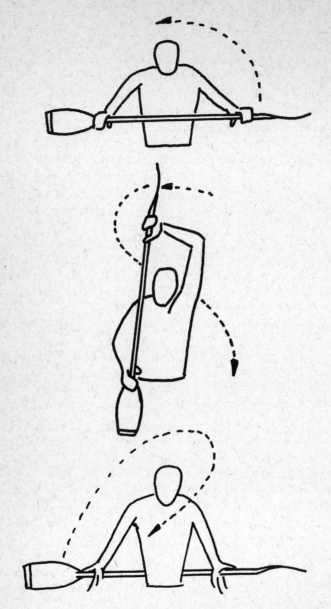

Shoulder excercises

down on the upper part of the shaft. This is designed to lock the arms and shoulders into one straight line. Squat slightly so that the knees are bent, the weight on the toes, and the backside sticks out in an undignified posture. With the trunk leaning forward one approximates to the sitting position in the canoe. Now, chin up and look for a mark on the wall or in the distance in line with the body straight ahead. Swing one paddle blade over the mark and then the other. Repeat, picking up speed with the swing and feel the surge of effort from the toes upwards. Work hard against oneself. The trunk should feel the effort below the ribs. Have plenty of room all around. If done with weights, start with 35 lb. on the bar, no more, and work up to heavier weights. Two minutes of this is quite enough even with a light paddle. The aim is to make it clear to novices that much of the driving force of the paddling action springs from the toes even with the shoulders locked and out of use.

Some may use a windmilling action of the paddle in order to practise feathering, but really this is of little use unless contact with the water is there to give true patterning of the muscles and nervous system.

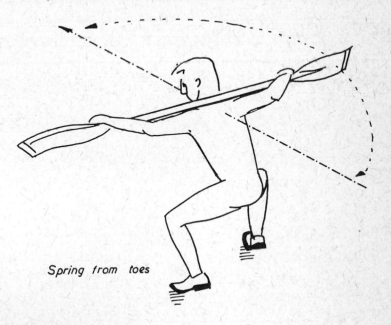

Spring from toes

Start of Scout LD race, River Arun. Note rudder swept over by rushing water, making handling difficult. The young man with spectacles will have tied them on. Note jointed paddle shafts. These have a nasty habit of coming apart at the moment of maximum effort and stress, apart from the annoying loss of feathered angle if the ferrule is slack.

Chapter 4

The Lifejacket

BSS 3595   BSS 3595   BSS 3595.
The numbers given above should be remembered as the British
Standard Specification for the lifejacket. If you have responsibility
for others be sure that you know what lifejackets your charges
should wear, and make them wear them.

The purpose of the lifejacket is to keep mouth and nose above
water during normal water conditions as found whilst canoeing.
It is not absolutely safe. It is possible for people to drown whilst
wearing first-class lifejackets. There was the case of a boy wearing
a first-class lifejacket which held him in a weir stopper so that the
body oscillated every six or seven seconds, driven down by the
down-rush from the weir, lifted in the stopper by the lifejacket
and swept back under the downrush by the flow of the stopper.
Another case concerned two fishermen wearing lifejackets with
loose straps so that the lifejacket supported the bodies about a
foot under the surface. Use of a lifejacket is not an automatic
passport to safety. Knowledge of function and use in practice is
required.

A variety of supporting devices have been used. The lifebelt is a
classic example of what is *not* required. It supports the middle of
the body, so that the rescuers find a conscious person waiting
happily upright in the water, but an unconscious one probably
dead, hanging in the water head and feet down draped over the
supporting belt. Kapok lifejackets have been used, but these,
although better than the lifebelt, usually had as much buoyancy in
front as behind the body, and although the body was usually
found with the head on the surface there was always some doubt
as to whether the head would be face downward or upward. Usually
it would be face downward, mouth and nose immersed.

39

Experience led the Royal Air Force to devise the May West in which two substantial 'pillows' were contained within the jacket to support the chest and the back of the neck. The main point about the May West was that it was the first to support the body in the proper attitude in the water, chest upward, face forward, body at about 45 deg. to the horizontal in the water. It was, however, rather unsatisfactory for canoeing use. The RAF jacket was rarely used although often worn and was, therefore, usually dry, and kept in first-class condition; the metal screw valve was kept greased and the CD bottle charged and ready for use.

A group of young men were using rolled up lifejackets with CD bottles in them ready for instant use. When the lever was pressed the bottles were found to be discharged and the jackets did not inflate. It is impossible to know if a CD bottle is charged unless it is removed from the lifejacket for checking. When lifejackets are in constant use such checks leave too much to human error.

A man was using an orally inflated lifejacket during rolling practice. The trip lever for the bottle was caught during the roll and the bottle super-inflated the jacket which exploded under water; most spectacular, and expensive!

Dead or alive?

Dave Mitchell at Shepperton, showing the arrogant power of a master. No buoyancy aid; absence of crash hat indicates that this was not a competition photograph.

Lifejackets with gas bottle inflation have their place, as with sub-aqua swimmers who, one assumes, will give them proper attention with full knowledge of the necessary checks and responsibilities. Their use for canoeists is not recommended.
Canoeists have varying attitudes to lifejackets. Those in the coaching scheme are very conscious of the possibility that one day they may be required to face the coroner and answer searching questions. Slalom canoeists quite reasonably point out that the use of full size lifejackets in the turbulent waters which they frequent may in fact inhibit paddling actions when free paddle actions are essential for survival, because to leave the canoe is always a move for the worse. Sprint and racing canoeists will object to using a full lifejacket, or even any lifejacket, as they quite rightly point out that its use inhibits an efficient racing paddle action. One must make a decision about lifejackets in view

Start of sprint C1 race. These racing shells are the most unstable canoeing devices ever produced; skill in balancing is very necessary. Note shaft bending under savage thrust. Absence of life-jackets is typical of sprinters, but not to be admired by novices. These people are very expert in a highly specialised branch of the sport.

of what one wishes to do with canoes. My ambition is to see everyone using a suitable lifejacket as a matter of course; it will not be realised until the demands of the various types of canoeing use have had their effect on lifejacket design and that won't happen until all canoeists wear lifejackets and make constructive criticisms of them.

Meanwhile, young people see their heroes using canoes in rough water without lifejackets and the idea of wearing lifejackets may never occur to them.

Development of lifejackets for constant use by water sportsmen was given a real push by an article in *Which* a few years ago, criticising some lifejackets in no uncertain terms. The Canoeing National Coach wrote an article in the June 1964 issue of *Canoeing in Britain* about the physical requirements of lifejackets and Surgeon Commander Davidson, MB, ch.B, RN, described the requirements of a good lifejacket in the July 1963 issue of the magazine *Canoeing*. It is fair to say that the most important developments took place early in 1964 when certain firms developed a lifejacket suitable for canoeing use. There have been difficulties since then; for example, materials of inferior quality being made up into lifejackets which did not stand up to normal canoeing usage. These teething troubles are being dealt with so that almost any lifejacket of the type which has the BSS 3595 and kite mark approval is now suitable for canoeing use.

Some difficulties were experienced with materials which rotted when exposed continually to strong sunlight or when greasy hair oil was rubbed onto the collar pieces. Some valves slipped out of the inflation tubes, others allowed water to dribble into the jacket when a capsize took place so that the lifejacket filled up over a period of weeks. Others had open cell pads inside them for 'solid' buoyancy and these absorbed water thus reducing the effective buoyancy of the lifejacket. Recent lifejackets have a new valve which will not leak but it requires a fair puff to blow air into it initially. The shape of the front air bag, in particular, is a matter for very careful design—if the bag is made narrow to allow the arms free movement it must be made longer to obtain the required amount of buoyancy. Small people using such a lifejacket found that the lower edge of the bag and its corners rubbed on parts of the canoe. This chafed the material and caused leaks.

Vertical acceleration

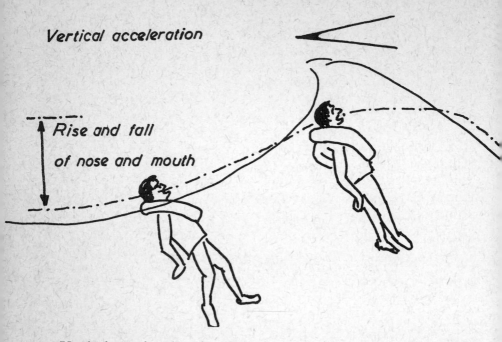

Rise and fall of nose and mouth

Vertical acceleration in choppy waves is an important factor especially in enclosed waters where waves cannot build up long wavelengths, but can develop considerable amplitude. A short very choppy wave condition will require a body, which may weigh 12 stones, to be lifted up so that the nose and mouth will clear the wave top and then flop back into the trough every four or five seconds. Vertical acceleration is a function of the weight of the body, the density of the water, the volume of the buoyancy immersed and the rate at which it must operate.

In order to ensure sufficient vertical lift, then, the volume of the lifejacket should be increased. This has certain physical limits: the size of the bag on the chest must not be greater than that dictated by the width of the chest and the distance at which the paddle operates in front of the body. Its length must be limited too, as has been shown. If the front bag is limited in size, it is not possible to increase the size of the lifejacket at the back, as this will have the effect of turning the body on to its face; present lifejackets must turn the body face upwards within five seconds. The relationship between front and rear buoyancy is critical.

Therefore, it has been found that lifejacket design is restricted and that it must be a compromise. The Board of Trade lifejackets as used in the Merchant Navy are very large but far too bulky for canoeing use. This lifejacket does not need to be used very often and then for supporting the body in the water or for boat drill. The RNLI lifejacket has three stages, oral inflation, solid pads and gas bottle inflation. It is bulky, costly and is designed to support the wearer *and* the person being rescued.

The purpose of these comments is to show that lifejackets may be within the requirements of the BSS 3595, and yet be not quite what is required by the canoeing user.

Lifejacket canvas covers have been made to reduce frictional wear to the air bag and to keep off the rays of the sun among other

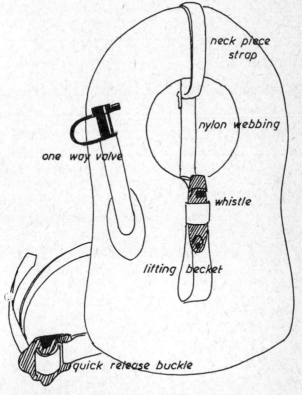

LIFEJACKET BSS 3595

benefits. Such a cover is more comfortable to wear and this is important when one's chin is in close contact with the material. The cover may have pouches stitched to it to take flares for sea use. The cover can hold whistle, compass and other small items usually carried in the pouch on the front of an anorak, which may not be accessible because of the presence of the lifejacket. Finally, painted monograms to indicate ownership may, with safety, be applied to the front of a cover when some paints may damage the proofing material on the air bag. Covers are said to extend the life of the lifejacket by a factor of three. Lifejackets in constant use without covers may last only six months.

A SUGGESTED SPECIFICATION FOR A CANOEING LIFEJACKET

1. BSS 3595. Kite marked.
2. Correct shape.
3. Two-stage 'solid' pads and air inflation.
4. Bright orange colour.
5. Straps of nylon or other rotproof material and strong lifting becket.
6. Buckles of strong rustproof steel.
7. Neck strap to hold neck piece down out of line of sight over shoulder.
8. Buoyancy pads in chest and neck sections to be made of closed cell material.
9. Chest bag 12 in. deep, 12 in. across, 4 in. thick.
10. Neck pad fixed into position by pockets *not* free to wander about neck section.
11. Bottom corners of bag well rounded to avoid frictional damage.
12. Material similar to 'Hyperlon', a synthetic fibre material with a synthetic and not natural rubber proofing.
13. Valve tight fit in inflation tube. It should enter $1\frac{1}{4}$ in.
14. Valve cap substantial and resistant to chewing.
15. Deflated buoyancy: 16 to 20 lb.
16. Inflated buoyancy: not more than 40 lb. and not less than 35 lb.

17. Plastic whistle attached (cold metal skins lips).[1]
18. Cover for comfort, personal additions and identification.

SPRAY DECK

The spray deck is essential to any canoeing. One should never go onto the sea without one. Its purpose is to seal the gap between body and cockpit hole. It must do this even when many stones weight of water thumps down onto it during, say, a surfing session. A buoyant lively canoe can be controlled but a canoe with several gallons of water slopping about inside will destroy the balance.

The spray deck brings with it problems. Because it must maintain a good seal during difficult conditions, it will not release easily until one part of the elastic cuff is caused to spring off the cockpit rim. The best place for this to happen is over the knees. Once the seal has been broken the water pressure outside which is trying to push the spray deck and paddler down into the cockpit will equalise the pressure inside. The pressures will not equalise until the spray deck is lifted from the rim. Cold fingers scrabbling at a half-inch gap half-inch deep may be unable to seize the spray deck cuff and lift it out. This is where the release strap helps. The strap, or better, cord, should be looped at either end around the cockpit rim cuff elastic and spliced back onto itself. People are unlikely to help themselves to a handy length of cord if it is spliced and not simply knotted.

---

[1] I have heard recently of an expert looping in surf who found he could not at first use his paddle to roll. The shaft was trapped close to his chest because the whistle on its thin cord had slipped from its pouch and had whipped around the shaft, holding it. He broke the cord and lost his whistle as he rolled.

Chapter 5

Basic Paddling Strokes

The variety of strokes one may use is vast. A paddle movement will have an effect on the movement of the canoe which entails changing to another paddle movement in midstroke and this stroke in turn may have to be modified almost immediately. The strokes which are given here are rarely used exactly as one would practise them; nevertheless, it is by practising them that sensitivity to the feel of the blade in the water is developed.

The drills here suggested are worth regular practice so that one may attempt to extend the nervous system right down to the tips of the paddle blades. This is rather a dramatic statement but it does reflect my view that the paddle should be thought of as an extension of the body.

By regular practice one may begin to identify the component parts of actions used by experts when paddling and it is rather satisfying to watch an expert at work and know exactly what he is doing. Having analysed the moves one may find a slight improvement in one's own handling of the paddle.

The basic skills are given first. They are those which the British Canoe Union require for the Proficiency Certificate tests and are based on the touring canoeist's requirements for satisfactory handling of the canoe. These skills have been in use for many years and they should be regarded as a sound base from which to start.

Over the years many touring canoeists have become slalom canoeists, which has led to a rapid development of new skills. The slalom Canadian canoe, a development of the traditional canoe, offered a much greater variety of strokes with the single bladed paddle than the simpler double ended kayak paddle. However, it is easy to see that the double ended paddle is simply two single bladed paddles joined together. The single bladed skills could be, and were, transferred to kayak handling, and so variety was increased.

New materials in canoe building, such as glass reinforced plastic, allowed canoes to be used on rougher and rougher waters with less chance of destruction in the turbulent churn of froth and water over rocks. The rougher the water becomes the deeper down is the solid water. The surface layer of the water is so shot through with air that the blade no longer grips as it should so deeper water must be dug for and found if blades are to grip and do their job. This too has changed the principles of paddling.

Improved building techniques and design have also had their effect as narrower canoes require more skill to balance them. I remember thinking how lean and long and racy looking was a canvas canoe 15 ft. long by 28 in. beam—but that was ten years ago. Because canoes are narrower, paddle shaft length is less because one does not need the long paddle to reach to the water far out over the sides of the wide canoe. Long paddles of course meant an almost horizontal paddle shaft in use and blade depth was just under the surface. The narrow canoe—24 in. wide or less—allows the shaft to be used almost vertically and so the blade may seek deep water. The recommendation in books used to be, 'The blade should only just be immersed and the shaft held at an angle that just clears the coaming—lifting too high is a common beginner's fault.' Well, I'm about to recommend a whole succession of common beginner's faults—by previous standards!

Paddling forward

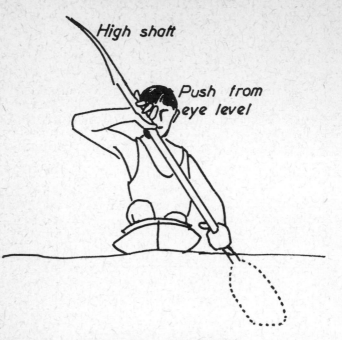

PADDLING FORWARD

The first principle is that one puts the blade into the water on one side of the hull, pushes and pulls on the shaft, and levers the canoe and body past the blade. When the canoe-body unit has passed, the blade must be lifted out and the other blade dropped into the water, the action repeated on the other side, and so on. Don't try to teach a beginner all the following points at once or he won't grasp them. Just let him potter about on the water and at first don't say anything about his execrable style. I find that the following eight points just about cover the necessity for good style.

1. *Keep the paddle shaft as close to the upright as possible*

Place the paddle far out from the canoe (as in a sweep turn) and try to make progress forward. You will find yourself moving in a series of gentle swerves. It may be demonstrated by the use of the triangle of forces that a sideways force is introduced every time the canoe turns and so a swerving movement is begun. The impossible ideal would be to place the blade right on the centre line of the canoe!

S. Jackson, in a 'Hunter' K1, made in Denmark, price well over £100. Note longer paddle shafts used by sprinters, and assymetrical blades. These paddles cost about £12 compared with paddle kits at about £2.

Alistair Wilson, Ayrshire Kayak Club, in a wooden 'Pointer' a type which really changed the sprint racing scene. He has been the fastest man in Britain in his time. His paddles are probably made by his own firm. The thrust for paddling comes all the way from the toes.

Therefore, viewed from the front the shaft should swing from an angle of about 80 deg. to the horizontal on one side to an angle of 80 deg. to the horizontal on the other. The centre of the shaft should remain about over the centre line of the canoe.

2. *Clip the blade out of the water as it is level with the hip*

If the blade carries backward beyond the hip, the forward angle of the shaft must mean that the drive face of the blade becomes angled upwards and the continuation of this stroke means that, as it swings backwards and upwards, it is lifting water. The upward lift applied so far behind the centre of gravity causes the stern to be depressed and so the canoe develops a bobbing action as each blade reaches the back of its swing. This see-saw motion is a most inefficient way of propelling the canoe.

As the blade dips into the water, obtains its grip sliding the canoe hull alongside, clip the blade out neatly to the side. It should chop out with a crisp plucking noise like a high-flung stone dropping spinning into water. The smart clipping out of the blade on one side drops the other blade ahead into the water ready for use. It also throws water off the shaft reducing drips onto the paddler.

3. *Open the fingers on the forward push*

Grip the shaft firmly with the fingers curled about it and place the blade as far forward as possible. Now open the fingers and see how the blade moves forward another four to six inches. This lengthens the 'stride' of the paddle on each stroke.

The opening of the fingers requires that the grip on the shaft should be relaxed. This is probably only possible on fairly calm water as rough water causes such a kick about that a free-flying shaft may be the result of this action. It is necessary to snatch the shaft at the precise moment of entry into the water. It is almost as if the blade is thrown ahead into the water and the snatch is made as one catches up with it. Practice this where a missed snatch will not have serious consequences.

4. *At one point of each stroke both arms must be straight*

Unskilled paddlers are often seen with the paddle shaft clutched close to their chests, and arms bent resulting in awkward action and painful shoulders. The body has much more strength than the arms so swing the body with the action. The arms bend only slightly at the start of the thrust and at the end of the swing. At the beginning of the stroke the lower arm is straight and the upper arm flexed. The upper arm straightens in a punch action from eye level down to the bows; both arms are now straight until the lower arm flexes to clip the blade out of the water. Try to keep both arms straight for as long as possible. One knows that proper paddling is developing when the ache of unused muscles leaves the shoulders and moves to the inner part of the thighs. Practice removes even this ache and a lovely easy swinging action results.

5. *Always lean forward when paddling forwards*

It is a good rule to lean into the movement in whatever direction one goes. Going forward: lean forward. This is why backrests have been out-dated by better skills. However, I must confess that on long paddles I lean back and slump from time to time. The aim should be to place the paddle blade as far forward as is possible on each stroke.

L. Oliver, who represented Britain at Mexico, in training at Pangbourne. Note raised knee and almost straight arms, paddle about to chop out level with hips. Thrust is being transferred to canoe by left leg kick balanced by right arm push, left arm pull. Note rich blood supply to biceps and triceps developed by years of weight training and paddling.

Keith Wickham. Heading for some surging fall on the Dee at Llangollen, 1968. The face, a snarl of effort, indicates that only the utmost is good enough at the top of the slalom divisions in Britain. Keith began canoeing in about 1963 in Sunderland docks in a canvas and lath canoe. He is now an international paddler, representing Britain.

6. *Keep your knees together*

Paddle racing people have a long wide cockpit so that they may bring their knees together and avoid the unsettling and limiting grip of the knees on the coaming frame or the under-deck knee braces which are used in W/W canoes.

My type of canoeing requires rough water handling in all directions. I can imagine a long wide cockpit canoe in a surf loop allowing its occupant to catapult far out ahead of the smash. A W/W canoe would wheel over all in one piece with the paddler quite at home and in full control of the fun. Each type of canoe offers its particular brand of enjoyment: racing canoes, speed and easy efficient paddling; W/W types, control in accidents.

With the knees together one is able to drive the footrest forward with the foot on the side that has the blade in the water. This results in each knee flexing in turn and much of the drive of the action comes from the toes upwards.

7. *The seat should be as high as one can manage without sacrificing all the stability of the hull*

Obviously, the higher the seat the fewer will be able to remain in the canoe as it is raised. But those who do will find that they can place more power into the action thrusting the paddle down and forward. It is said that it takes a racing paddler almost a year to attune his paddling style to his canoe and paddles. He raises and lowers his seat, compares times over the sprint distances, tries bigger blades, smaller blades, longer and shorter shafts, all the time tuning up to maximum performance, until he knows that his position in the canoe is correct to a quarter of an inch both for forward and upward reach, his knees bent by just the right amount, and so on.

8. *Don't see-saw*

There are various reasons for this action—one has already been mentioned on page 52. The danger is that one is tempted to hurl the whole weight of the body forward in order to put the paddle further forward and to heave the canoe forward by lunging backwards onto the rearward paddle. A smooth steady progress is required with a light, quick action. Do not give way to the desire to surge along.

Most of these points apply to the novice paddler and should be constantly remembered especially on long paddles when shoulders droop, heads hang forward onto lifejacket tops and the paddle splays out from the canoe in a weak sloppy move. Correct action under stress produces real learning and understanding.

BRAKES

1. Sitting still, drop one blade into the water, back of the blade to ·the front and held at right-angles to the cockpit.
2. Lift it out, turn shaft through 90 deg. and put the other blade into the water with the back of the blade forward and shaft at right-angles to cockpit.
3. Lift out of the water, put the other blade out behind the cockpit and sweep it forward through the water in a short (3 ft.) arc, as deep as possible.
4. Lift the blade out of water and repeat on other side.
5. Start the canoe moving forward and repeat very gently. Ensure that blade angles are correct every time since a forward swing with the lower edge of the blade leading the top edge will result in a deep slice and a capsize.
6. Build up speed until the action is a twelve-stroke sprint and a four-stroke stop with white water thrashing about in great gouts of foam.
7. To be really skilful, learn how to stop without the white water thrash by using the deep blade and a much more powerful and efficient action.
8. Do not rotate the shaft so that the drive face is forward. Braking must be an emergency action and there simply is not time in an emergency to rotate the shaft. Develop the good habits early. Dithering indecision has its penalties.

PADDLING BACKWARDS

1. Turn shoulders and body to the side on which the blade first enters. Try to put the blade in as far back as possible.
2. Lean back.
3. Heave down and forward on shaft and shove the blade forward toward the bows.
4. Chop the blade out early, about level with knees.
5. Turn body to the other side and repeat.

Dave Mitchell; British National Champion, silver medallist World Championships, 1967. The master in a thoughtful move. Judging by curve of bending shaft, he is thrusting in fast reverse through gate. What colour will the pole be that is visible in this picture, assuming that he is going the right way through?

6. On still water, as speed over the water is built up, the canoe will be found to swing one way or the other and correction is better done by a reverse bow rudder moulded into the paddling stroke.

TURNING STROKES—SWEEP TURN

The turn is done by putting the blade out on the water as far from the canoe as possible, keeping the shaft low. It can be done left or right, with a forward or backward action. A forward action on one side is alternated with a reverse action on the other side to provide the forward and reverse sweep turn in which the canoe is caused to pivot more or less on the spot. A forward sweep turn repeated will not only turn the canoe but progress it around the rim of a circle rather than about a pivoting point. The forward and reverse sweep has advantages in a restricted space.

1. Extend paddle. Place the forward blade beside and touching bows, drive face turned outwards.
2. Lean forward. Sweep the blade across water in a big swinging arc.
3. As the blade swings tilt upper edge so that it leads the action. This gives a slight planing action which may be used for support.
4. Bring the blade back to touch canoe hull at stern. To do this, swing the body with turn and pull backward with rear arm. Thrust across the body with the other arm so that the paddle shaft lies parallel to hull on the action side.

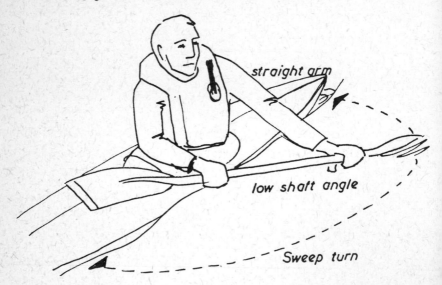

straight arm

low shaft angle

Sweep turn

5. Take care not to trip over the paddle blade. It must clip neatly out of the water just as it reaches the hull. If it is trapped against the hull by the interaction of the hull's swing and the water pressure against the blade there is a tendency to roll and the blade is trapped and not available for balance.

6. This describes a forward sweep turn. The rate of turn may be increased if the waterline length of the canoe is reduced by lying over onto the side of the canoe and using the 12 in. rocker of the gunwale line to ease the turn. The angled blade in its sweep is used for support.

7. A reverse action uses the back of the blade to take the water pressure, and one simply reverses the action described in 1 to 6 above.

8. A slight improvement to the action may be obtained when the blade (on either a forward or reverse move) is at the bows, by lifting the shaft across the face into the bow rudder position, upper hand knuckles touching opposite shoulder.

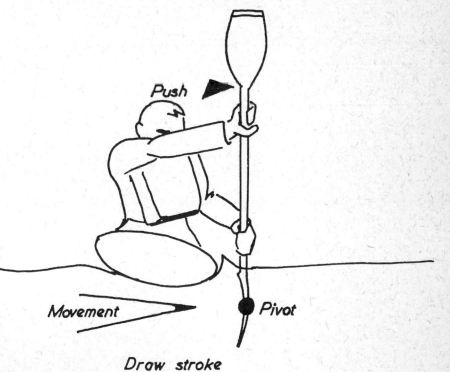

Draw stroke

DRAW STROKE

The need to make the canoe to go sideways is often very great in rough water in order to avoid obstacles. In that case the high draw is used, a stroke in which the distinction between draw and support becomes blurred. At this time I really wonder whether it is necessary to produce two distinct actions, a draw and a support, when in fact the very best and most powerful support stroke on a vertical shaft is also the very best and most powerful draw stroke. However, at the beginner stage it is probably better to emphasise the distinction. Start very gently until blade release is reliable.

1. Place the paddle in a normal grip, blade drive face down onto water, shaft at right-angles to cockpit and held low.
2. Dip the blade down into the water, thrust shaft across body with upper hand and turn body toward blade in water.
3. Pull the shaft close to the canoe with lower hand.
4. Just before the canoe over-rides the blade, rotate the shaft through 90 deg. and slip the blade through the water back to the beginning position.

SCULLING DRAW

All sculling actions are similar, except that the resultant thrust is directed in different ways. The blade generates power by deflecting masses of water rather than by providing a fulcrum for a lever. The basic practice described here applies to all actions. It is necessary to understand which part of the blade is which.

1. First practice strokes inshore to obtain complete familiarity with the positions of the blades: the edge which leads the swing of the blade is called the leading edge; when the blade is in line with the swing the stroke is called a slice; when the blade is at right-angles to the swing it is said to be square.
2. Start with the slice angling the leading edge away from your feet. This requires that each swing is stopped at the end, the blade angle changed (as the leading edge is now the other edge of the blade) and the return swing commenced. The most effective angle of attack is about 30 deg. to the line of swing. The angle of attack is measured between the line through the width of the blade and the line of swing.
3. Try this in the canoe with the blade tip just clipping the water surface. Take the blade deeper as confidence is gained and try

pulling a leaf or floating object towards the blade by the action.

4. The action described in 2 and 3 deflects masses of water towards the feet so that, if the feet were free to move, they would move towards the blade.

5. If the angle of the blade is reversed so that the leading edge angles towards the feet, then the back of the blade will push water away and the blade will try to move towards the feet. This is the sculling push-over or pry.

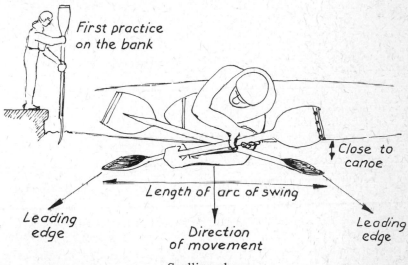

Sculling draw

6. Remember that the blade drive face is angled at all times towards the feet.

7. Check that standard grip maintained and check any tendency to reverse the grip of the upper hand.

8. If you find yourself persistently switching blade so that it alternately presents drive face and then back of blade to the canoe, hold the blade where it joins the shaft as if holding a table tennis bat. This will correct reversal of the blade face at the beginning. The drive face is towards the canoe.

9. As skill grows, and the swing becomes smooth and accurate, make your paddle dig deeper. Sink your lower hand into the water wrist deep without, of course, moving your grip on the paddle shaft which must be standard at this stage.
10. The upper hand knuckles should touch the opposite shoulder.
11. More power is obtained by using a contra-swing with the upper hand so that the centre of the paddle shaft remains almost pivoted at a fixed point, top and bottom blades oscillating at opposite ends of the diameter of a circle.

The action may be varied as follows: the line of thrust is measured at right-angles to the line of swing of the paddle at the centre of the swing. This is only at right-angles when the blade angle of attack is the same on each swing. The line of thrust may be applied forward of the centre of gravity by leaning forward or behind by leaning backwards.

The line of swing need not be parallel to the line of the canoe. It

Pauline Squires. Note crash hat, buoyancy aid, concentrated expression. See angle of left wrist (beginners tend wrongly to reverse grasp when practising this basic move).

may be set at an angle, in which case the line of thrust may be directed through the centre of gravity from an angled position resulting in an angled direction of movement.

The angle of attack of the blade as it swings may be varied, so that on the rearward swing it may be nearly slicing and on the forward swing it may be nearly square. In that case a sideways movement, with the bows leading in a steady turn, will result.

Remember the three basic variables:

1. Point of intersection of line of thrust and line of canoe.
2. Angle of intersection of line of thrust and line of canoe.
3. Angle of attack of blade.

When the basic idea of a sideways draw has been mastered play around with the variables and produce the myriad moves possible.

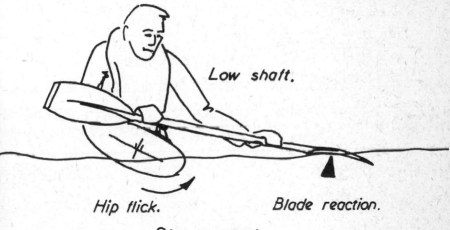

Low shaft.

Hip flick.   Blade reaction.

Slap support.

SLAP SUPPORT

I don't like this description as it tempts people to whang down the blade onto the water producing a crack like a 0.22 and occasionally, a shattered shaft. The slap idea is all very well to start the beginner off but stop it as soon as possible.

1. Take the shaft in the standard grasp, drive face down and blade pushed out to one side about two feet from surface of water, shaft nearly level.

2. Slap the blade face down onto the water and feel the reaction kick-back along the shaft.
3. Begin again, rolling over towards the blade, slap down and regain balance using reaction in shaft.
4. Now place the blade just under the water surface so that the blade has grip both upwards and downwards.
5. Progress in stages so that the elbow dips into water before balance is regained, then the shoulder, then dip the head in and regain balance. Beginners should dip elbow quite easily but it will take some practice to dip the head and regain balance. Practising hip-flick (see rolling) should assist here.

SCULLING SUPPORT

The sculling action is used but in this case the reaction from the planing blade is used in a vertical direction and not for a sideways movement.

1. Position as in 1 for slap support. Start sculling swing across the surface of the water, leading edge angled upwards slightly, angle of attack 30 deg. or less and drive face downwards.
2. Start to lean out onto the planing blade.
3. Progress from wet elbow to wet shoulder to position where the head is turned upwards to the air and the canoe is laid over, bottom upwards, over 90 deg. from level position. Regain balance by use of hip-flick. This takes a lot of practice.

Chapter 6

Advanced Paddling Strokes

There has been for some time a difficulty in deciding what is an advanced paddling stroke. Some of the strokes described here may be basic to some while others, for example the forward paddling stroke described in the chapter on basic canoeing strokes, may be well in advance of what others have been using for years.

The aim should be to equip the paddler, by regular practice of certain moves, with the ability to tackle almost any situation he is likely to meet with natural ease and properly conditioned reflexes. In emergency there is no time to think before acting.

Based on the theory that each person is a body, a mind and a spirit, each combined into a personality which is individual, then I would wish to develop:

1. A flexible, powerful body ready at once to do what the mind requires.
2. A flexible resourceful mind ready to comprehend at once every change in the situation and to act upon it.
3. A spirit so strengthened by experience that it remains constant in its purpose and achieves it no matter what body and mind must suffer.

However, being human I fall short of these standards. Certainly experience gives one the power to do better next time. Never play the hero by trying to prove that the impossible is possible and endangering others in the ensuing disaster.

OVERSIDE ACTIONS

In a recent examination I asked the candidate to teach his class the overside draw stroke. 'Ha!' said he, 'Gimmicks!' Perhaps it is a gimmick, but I find that the effort of twisting the body voluntarily into an apparently impossible position lends power to deal with moments when the body *is* so twisted by water power. This is the first step toward the flexible body.

Overside draw

1. Hold the paddle in a normal grip.
2. Twist the body sideways so that the shoulder points are lined up as nearly as possible fore and aft.
3. Keep the shaft horizontal, held low down.

Overside draw

4. Put the rear blade into the water, 24 in. from side with the drive face inwards.
5. Pull the stern toward the blade.
6. Lift out the blade, do not over-ride.
7. Put the forward blade into the water, 24 in. from side with the drive face inwards. You must really reach out for this.
8. Pull the bows towards the blade.
9. Frequent repetition each side is a good limbering-up exercise.

Overside push over

1. Action is as above but the blade starts beside the canoe and pushes it away from the blade, the back of which takes the water pressure. This is very difficult with the bow push-over.
2. Regular practice each side.

note straight arm giving extra leverage

Overside push over

Forward and reverse overside sweep turn

1. Position as for overside draw.
2. Alternate bow draw and stern push-over.
3. It will be found that there is a rhythm in this, the stern push-over following the bow draw more easily than the converse, as the body winds up and almost immediately unwinds.
4. This action usually results in an endways movement along the periphery of a circle as well as a turn, and in a reverse direction leaning outward.
5. One should try to look at the stern during this movement.
6. This action may be done left and right with bow draw and stern push-over, and then with stern draw and bow push-over. The latter is very difficult.
7. You may never use this as a distinct movement but it is a stage programming of your body-mind computer.

PADDLE RUDDERS

Bow rudder

1. Take the paddle in a normal grip across canoe.
2. Place the right blade alongside right of bows with the drive face inward.
3. Right arm should be almost straight, fingers extended.

Bow rudder

4. Left blade is lifted across the face, over head and laid above right shoulder.
5. Back of forearm presses on forehead.
6. Do not reverse grasp of upper hand.
7. Dig blade deeper as confidence grows.
8. Practise left and right.
9. Move canoe forward slowly. Dip blade in lightly and turn toward blade.

C1 work in rough water. Note how the body is turned and the centre of the forehead used as a pivoting point. The old fashioned hand behind neck action limits freedom of movement of paddle. Top hand is control hand, palm over handgrip, thumb under.

10. Experiment: place blade further out, close in angle blade, upper edge outward, inward.
11. Try it faster as confidence is gained. Dig deep.
12. Try it backwards.

Cross bow rudder

1. Hold the paddle in a normal grasp across canoe.
2. Place left blade across bows and into water at right side of bows.
3. Look backwards towards the stern. There should be a considerable twist on the body.
4. Drive face towards the canoe. Reach round as far as possible and then more. This is where overside action practice helps.
5. Knuckles of right hand should rub the point of your right shoulder or side and rear deck of the canoe.
6. Move forward slowly increasing speed with practice. Dig deep.

Cross bow rudder

7. If control is lost the action 'locks on' and may be released by rotating the shaft until the upper edge of the blade angles forward and inwards.
8. Experiment: try it fast and slow, forward and backward, rotating shaft this way and that, both sides.
9. Note that in the bow rudder position one obtains the cross bow rudder position simply by bringing the upper blade forward and down into the water and by putting the forward blade back over the shoulder; *or*, by keeping it low and below waist level rather like the overside draw position.

Stern rudder

1. Take up the position as for overside action.
2. Put the rear blade into water, about 24 in. from side with the drive face inward.

3. Gather speed, drop blade into water and hold it firmly 24 in. out.
4. The canoe turns and, if of the slalom variety, will then skid along the line of the blade edge. The turn rapidly becomes ineffective.

HANGING ACTIONS

Draw turn

This move develops the bow rudder towards the hanging draw so one should practise this action immediately following the bow rudder practice and follow it with the hanging draw.
1. Take up bow rudder position.
2. Bring the blade back alongside the cockpit, shaft vertical and blade close to canoe.
3. The blade drive face should be inward with the leading edge angled outwards.

Draw turn

4. Gather speed, drop the blade into water and hold on tight.
5. The canoe swings around paddle and also moves to that side, hence the name, draw-turn.
6. Experiment: fast and slow, forward and backward, right and left, more or less angle on the blade, blade close in and further out from canoe.

Hanging draw

1. Position as for the draw turn. Take the blade further back until the body is turned to the side, lower arm almost straight and upper arm braced so that the forearm is across the forehead.

Hanging draw

Dave Mitchell, in a high draw come high speed turn. Compare wrist action with that of Pauline Squires on page 62.

2. Drive face should be inwards, leading edge angled outward with the blade about 18 in. from side.
3. Gather speed, drop in blade and lean onto it. The drag on one side tends to turn the canoe to that side but the angled blade deflects water under the stern and the reaction pulls the stern across. The aim is to make the canoe move off sideways still pointing in the same direction.
4. Experiment: blade left and right, faster and slower, action far back and almost up to cockpit, blade close in and far out, blade angle ranging from slicing to square.
5. As skill increases and the direction in which the canoe points is controlled, lean further out onto blade so that one is almost supported on the vertical shaft, sustained in its vertical position by the thrust from the angled blade deep down. Finish with 'big-digs' draw and hip-flick.
6. This action is very useful in fast water for quick avoidance of obstacles and for really classy demonstrations of how to come alongside when impressing the examiner. Don't fluff it though— it looks ludicrous! The action is that used by single-bladed paddlers for stopping the way of a Canadian without changing direction.
7. Practise this one constantly—it is particularly useful.

High telemark

1. Take up the bow rudder position with the blade far out, almost at right-angles to the canoe.
2. The drive face should be inward and forward with the shaft high.
3. Gain speed.
4. Lay the canoe over onto the blade so that the upper forearm is laid across the forehead.
5. Dig deeper as speed is gained, lie further over and gain upthrust from the deep set blade—the angle must be right, of course.
6. The canoe spins around the blade. The rate of turn is increased the further out one can place the blade. Imagine the canoeist right way up with the paddle held in normal grasp high above head and both arms straight (a 'Geronimo'). Now lay him over at right-angles with an ear in the water and you have the position.
7. This is of the greatest use in fast water where the bows move

High telemark

from a water flow in one direction into a water flow in another direction and the velocity difference of the streams may be as high as 12 m.p.h. Then the high telemark is easy (or one rolls, maybe!)

Vertical shaft support

This is the move to which I refer so often as being *the* best move of all for instant retrieval of balance. It is taken during the paddle stroke in the normal rhythm of paddling. Sometimes I call it the 'big digs' draw.

1. The position is almost the same as for the high telemark.
2. Take the paddle further back almost to the hanging draw position.
3. Lay back and over and dig the blade deep with the drive face directly towards the canoe.
4. Lay over onto the blade, ear in the water, hip-flick up.
5. Practise hip-flick again and again in lay back position.
6. Try again—concentrate on pulling your backside over the paddle blade.
7. Keep your head low and laid backwards.
8. This move may also be developed from constant practice of the storm roll.
9. It can also be done laid forward, slightly forward of the high telemark position, but it seems more difficult to me that way. In this case the head is kept low and forward until the canoe is on even keel.
10. Apart from being a support stroke this is also an excellent

draw stroke for lifting the canoe about three feet to one side or another in a moment. The paddle shaft remains vertical the whole time. It is kept there by the swiftness of the strike and the suppleness of the bodily movement.

11. Try rapid alternation from one side to the other, rocking from side to side.

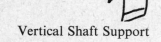

Vertical Shaft Support

Low telemark

This develops from the stern rudder and is also useful as a step towards the Colorado hook.

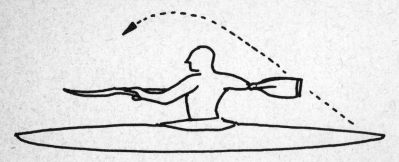

Low telemark

1. Take up a stern rudder position with the back of the blade forward and downward.
2. Make a reverse sweep-turn movement to bring the paddle close to the bows.
3. As speed increases lay further out onto blade and dig deeper.
4. The greatest power in the turn comes from laying the canoe right over so that one's head is almost in the water and the body weight largely on the planing paddle blade. With the weight transfer the canoe is less heavily loaded and thus turns more readily on the 12 in. rocker of the gunwale.

Colorado hook

This is useful for changing direction rapidly with one paddle move.

1. Cross bow rudder.
2. As speed of turn drops off drop the rearward blade into the water and move into a low telemark.
3. As balance is regained one may top off the lot with a change to a bow draw with the rearward blade as it moves forward past the median position. The wrists are dropped at once in order to rotate the drive face forward, and the bow draw is completed.
4. After the bow draw one is in position to drive off that blade into the sprint for whatever it is that one is aiming at. Strictly speaking, the Colorado hook is simply the cross bow rudder followed by the low telemark but the addition of the bow draw and the drive from the paddle in just the right position make it into a more useful action—four strokes off one blade in one move.
5. This is a very pretty move but a little impractical unless one uses it on really wild water. I link the four actions simply for the pleasure of turning figures of eight in a swimming pool.

Variations

The names of some of these are given below, and one may explore them at will. I once wrote a paper on these variations and decided that I really should try the lot just to be sure that I could. Anyway, away I went with two or three repetitions of each move. Very soon I was breathing hard, then sweating and finally gasping. I stopped to think about it and realised very suddenly that what I had suspected for some time was true—I am almost entirely right-handed, making most of the moves quite naturally on the right but struggling on the left. After an hour of steady work I had done most of the moves and was too tired to do any more! Try all these moves in all manner of ways and develop the flexible body and perhaps even a flexible mind.

SOME ALTERNATIVE STROKES

Stern bow rudder; bow stern rudder; reverse hanging draw; reverse high telemark; reverse turn-draw; reverse low telemark; vertical shaft support on the move, forwards, backwards.

PRINCIPLES TO REMEMBER IN PADDLE PRACTICE

1. Try forward, then backward.
2. Try left and right.
3. Alter shaft angles.
4. Alter blade angle of attack.
5. Place blade close to canoe.
6. Place blade far out from canoe.
7. Place blade well forward.
8. Place blade well back.
9. Try it sitting up, even keel.
10. Try it laid over, off balance, weight on blade.
11. Try it fast and slow.
12. Try some link-up that you have never seen used before. Be inventive. There may be some idea, some sequence of moves which suits you and no-one else.
13. Be flexible in body and mind; certain in spirit.

Chapter 7

Rolling Techniques

The lifejacket helps the person who has parted company with his canoe to keep nose and mouth above water but this is only a second line of defence. The better way to tackle any difficulty is to stay in the canoe. The canoe will turn itself upside down occasionally, but the skilled canoeist need have no fear of difficulty provided he rolls every time.

The 'Eskimo' roll has been regarded as an advanced skill but study of the movement of the canoe shows that it is in fact a basic and simple skill. Other paddle actions require more expertise. There is much to be said for teaching the novice to roll before tackling any other part of the sport. One word of caution—do not rely on the roll to take one out of difficulty and neglect to learn the canoeing skills correctly. One candidate for a Senior Instructor Award was advised to go away and learn to handle his paddle more effectively, even though he was able to roll almost anywhere, anytime. Nowadays the top class competitive canoeist in rough water no longer rolls as it is a waste of time—probably two seconds for each roll. A swift reflex action support stroke on a vertical paddle shaft is the expert's way out of difficulty.

Despite the warnings against using it every time, there is no doubt at all that rolling skill at once extends one's paddling ability and one's ability to learn to paddle effectively. It is one of the basic steps to full paddling skill.

There are several basic ways of rolling, as distinct from styles of rolling. The rolls may be performed with and without a paddle. They may be done laid forward or backward, down-left-up-right, or down-right-up-left; and that is without some of the variations, fancy or otherwise.

Which is the best way to learn to roll? That is not easy to answer, but consider the following situation: One is paddling along over rough water travelling faster than the water speed. Total overground speed may be 10 m.p.h. The bows then swing into a slack part—a backwater behind a rock where the water may be still or have a contrary movement. Let us say that the speed differential is 10 m.p.h. There is immediately a violent turning action in the horizontal plane linked with a violent turning over action and a capsize follows. The body and canoe have much kinetic energy and this must be lost by deceleration. The body plunges into the water and is effectively stopped in a moment. The canoe, now relieved of about half the weight of the paddler, runs on and tends to leave the body behind. The canoeist finds himself pressed up against the rear deck, face down and locked by the thighs into the canoe. This is desperate for novices, but ideal for rollers. The style known as 'Steyr' roll is perfect for this position. There is something to be said for teaching all novices the Steyr roll as a basic working stroke with other rolls and styles secondary to it. It is also important to be ambidextrous when rolling. Nevertheless, the first roll which I teach is the Pawlata which requires a laid forward position.

PAWLATA ROLL

The leading up drills are as follows:

Capsize

The basic capsize drill is learned or, in the case of skilled canoeists, practised as follows:
1. Lean forward.
2. Relax the legs.
3. Place the hands on each side of cockpit beside hips.
4. Take two deep breaths.
5. Capsize.
6. Wait (snort out air through nose to keep water out of facial sinuses).
7. Beat three times on the bottom of the canoe.
8. Forward roll out of cockpit.
9. Come up holding canoe in one hand, and paddle in the other.
10. Repeat with spray deck on.
11. Try for longer and longer delays, say ten seconds plus using a noseclip.

Assisted roll

This requires an assistant. It is not, strictly speaking, a roll but does give confidence both to the paddler and the assistant.

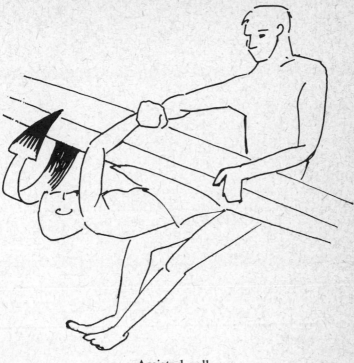

Assisted roll

1. Sit in the canoe with knees braced and spray deck on.
2. Lean forward and try to clasp the hands under the canoe.
3. Remaining in this position, capsize towards partner.
4. Partner at once takes hold of far gunwale of canoe and pulls paddler upright.
5. Check that paddler is still locked forward, hands under canoe.
6. Repeat. Paddler this time beats twice to show that he is under self control, and then waits as long as he feels he can—usually about 7 to 10 seconds. He then beats once more on the upturned hull and the partner at once rights him and the canoe. Wear a noseclip.

Hip flick drill

This is essential to the establishing of good rolling techniques. If the roll later shows six consecutive failures go back to this drill and use it as a reliable fall back position and exercise.

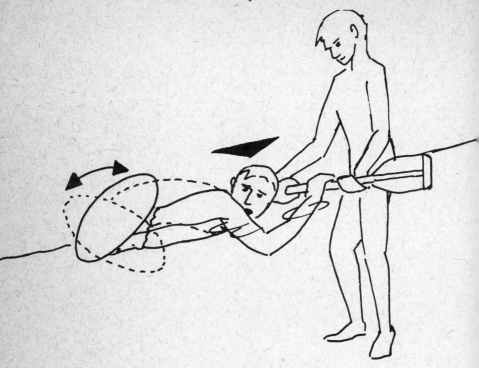

Hip flick drill

1. Lock into the canoe with spray deck on.
2. Place both hands on bath rail alongside.
3. Lie on the water, head just above water.
4. Partner may hold the paddle blade above the paddler's head to stop him lifting his head more than an inch or so above the surface. Let him breathe.
5. Tilt the canoe using hips until it flips over the point of balance.
6. By lunging upwards with the lower knee flick the canoe back onto balance. It is important NOT to raise the head.
7. Make this a rapid flick action, off balance-on balance.
8. Repeat, say, twelve times each side.

9. It is important that the partner checks that the paddler makes a distinct flicking action to bring the canoe on balance and that the movement springs from the middle and not the arms.

10. The purpose is to pattern the bodily movements into putting the canoe back onto balance first so that the body may be 'poured' back into position when canoe is on balance. Lifting the body first leads to struggles for balance.

Dry paddle drills

The first is to ensure that the paddle at least begins in the right position.

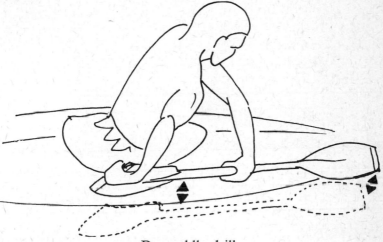

Dry paddle drill

1. Sit upright in the canoe hands on paddle so that the put-across position is used.
2. Wind up the paddle so that the rear wrist is turned outward and the forward hand and arm slightly flexed.
3. Check that the fore blade is tilted face upward and outward.
4. Fore blade must be held tightly onto the foredeck.
5. Place whole of paddle on the water surface alongside. Replace on deck.
6. Repeat, say, twelve times.

Wet paddle drill

This is further to ensure that the paddle begins its move correctly.

1. Take hold of paddle as in previous exercise.
2. Capsize.
3. Repeat the movement as in previous exercise, so that the paddle appears on the water surface alongside the canoe and parallel.
4. Replace the paddle on the foredeck which is under water.
5. Partner now rolls paddler up.
6. Check that fore paddle blade is in its proper position at the proper angle.

Dry paddle unwind

This exercise assists paddler in feeling the way that the arms and

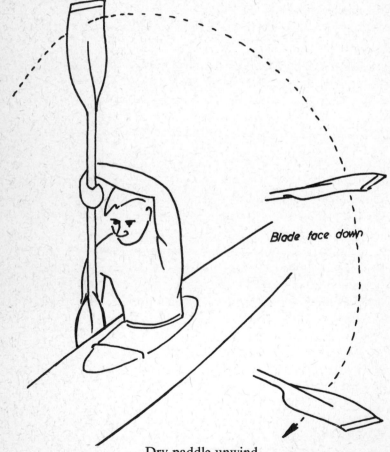

Blade face down

Dry paddle unwind

body move to make the strike when rolling (the associated roll of the canoe makes the move quite different when seen from the surface).

1. Wind up paddle.
2. Lean well forward.
3. Place paddle on the water alongside as described.
4. Lift off water in sweeping curve up over head so that the upper arm bicep rubs past the ear.
5. Keep the rearmost part of the swing about leve¹ with the cockpit.
6. Swing the paddle down onto water.
7. Tilt the leading edge of blade upwards and sweep it forward in a sculling movement across the surface of the water.

Wet paddle unwind

This is where the roll proper begins. Repeated practice and returns to the hip flick and paddle on-off drills should assist rolling after a short while. There are some, a very few, who roll first time after such a lead up. Others go through the lead up, fail several times, go back to fall-back drills and then rest. Fifteen minutes later they try again and succeed. This is mostly done by young men, aged from 15 to 18, who are physically fit, well built and water confident. Others will learn more slowly and require frequent repetitions of the orientation and confidence drills. Most of the power of rolling comes from learning to relax the muscles not needed for the action rather than bunching up every available fibre.

1. Sit in the canoe, locked in with spray deck on.
2. Wind up paddle. Check blade angle and shaft position.
3. Capsize.
4. Place paddle alongside.
5. STRIKE.
6. Don't think about it now.
7. Try six repetitions; if each is a failure go back to fall back drills.
8. Rest for fifteen minutes.
9. Try again.

FAULTS

1. *Paddle strikes across the canoe in the wrong direction.*
Go back to 'on-off' paddle drill—dry, then wet. An assistant can help by momentarily holding the paddle blade whilst pushing the

bows of the canoe away, thus putting the canoeist in correct attitude for the strike.

2. *Failure to wait before striking.*
As the canoe is turning over the strike begins. This results in the paddle slicing down deep, striking the bottom and not providing effective lift.

3. *Paddle angle wrong at start of strike.*
The paddler waits but his paddle blade angle is such that its outer edge is angled downwards and thus strikes and slices downwards as in fault 2. Do not confuse fault 2 with fault 3.

4. *Paddle not held firmly to foredeck as action begins.*
The blade drifts downwards off the deck of the upturned canoe before the strike begins. The strike is too low and ineffective.

5. *Paddle sets off correctly but immediately sinks too low.*
This is because the action is being taken too far forward. The full unwinding swing of the body and arm, so that the bicep rubs the ear, is not being used.

6. *Paddle sets off correctly but feels heavy and dead as it sinks to the bottom.*
This is the result of too much paddle angle. The angle of attack of the blade to the water is so steep that the blade is in a stalled position, loses lift from sculling action and simply sinks low. This sinking of the blade is characterised by its slowness and heaviness.

7. *The paddle sets off correctly but loses its angle of attack which becomes negative and the blade slips swiftly down to the bottom.*
This is similar to fault 3; it differs from 6 by its swiftness.

8. *Paddle and swing correct but paddler appears momentarily then falls back.*
This is failure to use the effective lift created by the skimming blade. I recommend a punch, a lunge with the knee and a predetermination to go hard for the roll.

9. *Paddler rises up, hovers, falls back. Canoe is noticeably not on balance.*
Go back to hip flick.

10. *Paddler swings paddle too far back, and is laid back at an angle, or remains sitting up straight. Laid back at an angle, his*

muscles don't work. Sitting up, his muscles are overloaded by the high rotational inertia of the body-canoe unit.

Sometimes the paddler will take naturally to the Steyr roll and this should be considered at this point. Many women seem to roll better when laid back along the rear deck. Sometimes they use a Pawlata wind-up to a Steyr roll. The important thing is to decide whether the paddler is to persist with the forward position of the Pawlata as described or transfer at once to the lay-back of the Steyr roll. In any event a sitting-up position is hopeless.

11. *Paddler rises up, canoe almost on balance, and then flops back.* Try using the reverse sculling action at the end of the stroke so that the planing paddle blade slips forward toward the bows whilst the last bit of balance is regained.

STEYR ROLL

This method is a laid-back roll with maximum leverage from the paddle. It differs from the Pawlata in that it sets off backwards.

Capsize

Repeat the drills already explained on page 78.

Assisted roll

1. Sit in the canoe, locked in with spray deck on and partner alongside.
2. Lay back so that rear of cockpit digs into spine.
3. Capsize towards partner. Lay back and press head up against deck.
4. Partner turns paddler upright. Note how little effort is required.
5. As paddler comes up, check that his head is touching the rear deck.

Hip-flick drill

1. Take up position alongside bath rail with both hands on rail.
2. Reach far back and lay head back. It will be found that only one hand can grasp the rail—the hand nearest to the rail when sitting up.
3. Take canoe off balance using hip movements. Hold head above water with hand on rail and *make* head touch rear deck.
4. Swing spare hand up and over gunwale of canoe towards rear.

Marsh Lock, Henley. Competition slalom kayaks in repose. Judging by the prevalence of KW 3s, and deep hulled boats, the photograph was taken about 1965–1966. Low rear deck boats are now necessary for the lay back roll, particularly the Steyr.

5. Keep back of head down near water and swing canoe back onto balance.
6. Repeat twelve times, both sides, off balance-on balance.

Note. In the Pawlata one looks down into the water during this exercise, but in the Steyr one looks upwards.

Dry paddle drills

1. Hold paddle in maximum lever position. (Put across)
2. Lock into the canoe with spray deck on and partner alongside.
3. Wind up paddle forwards then swing back over the shoulder on that side.
4. Lay back along deck so that paddle blade is resting either on the deck or on the water beside the canoe. It must not cross the canoe. The hollow face of the blade is uppermost, outer edge down.
5. The elbow of the hand which holds the inner blade is turned uncomfortably inwards towards the chest. The arm holding the shaft is crooked across the face; mouth and chin are jammed into crook of the elbow. The position is much easier when upside down and fully laid back with body partly supported by the water.
6. Look at the rear paddle blade by turning the head sharply to that side, looking round and backward. This really does require a degree of body twist which is uncomfortable sitting up but easy upside down.

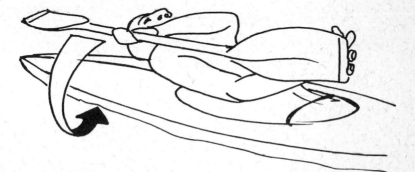

Dry paddle drill

Wet paddle unwind

The position is so difficult to adopt above water that dry unwinding of the paddle is unreal. The better way is to go for a half roll, that is, down one side and up the same side to begin with.

1. Take up the starting position.
2. Capsize away from the paddle.
3. Assistant catches the blade and holds it, checking the capsize.
4. Paddler checks blade angle, leading edge tilted upwards.
5. Strike (assistant releases blade), swing blade forwards and keeping head pinned back to deck.
6. If this fails go back to hip-flick drill on the rail.
7. When this is successful the partner need no longer interrupt the capsize.
8. Capsize and roll up as practised.
9. When this is successful, capsize *towards* paddle and complete roll.
10. At all times strive to press the head back against rear deck.

Note. Most paddlers seem to find difficulty in orienting under water when face downwards.

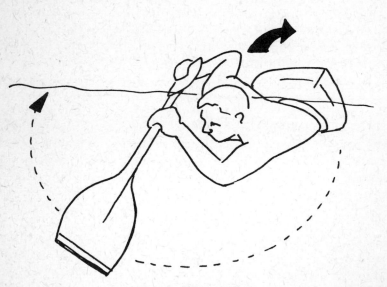

Wet paddle unwind

STORM ROLL

Some paddlers seem to find it easier to swing the paddle deep in the strike, and they persist in doing it instead of swinging it wide just under the surface as the Pawlata method requires. The storm roll may suit them better:

1. Take up the initial position as for Pawlata but with blade angle exactly at right-angles to the Pawlata position.
2. The hollow face of the blade is angled inwards and slightly upwards; the tip of the blade is almost vertical.
3. Dry paddle action requires the paddle to be placed deep into the water forwards. When the inverted position is used the fore blade whips up out of the water just before the strike.
4. The dry strike is directly up over the head and the swing away from the canoe is not used. When viewed from the surface it looks quite different, but that is how it feels.
5. Capsize and whip the blade up out of water.
6. STRIKE, hauling hard with the forward arm up over the head, initially.
7. The hip-flick should be a really snappy action, the whole sequence being a jerk rather than a swing.
8. The roll is quick and, when finished, the paddle shaft should be straight down in the water alongside. It is very like the support on a vertical shaft using maximum leverage.
9. It is so quick that faults have little time to develop. The main fault is that of incorrect blade angle. Too much blade angle and it ends up as a poor Pawlata; too little and the blade crosses the canoe and no lift is possible; correctly done it is effortless.

SCREW ROLL

The screw roll is simply a Pawlata or storm roll with a shortened lever. The position is identical except that the hands are in the normal grasp position on the paddle shaft. This roll requires a reliable hip-flick and exact timing.

PUT ACROSS ROLL

This is the method that used to be taught and it lends itself to being broken down into easy stages. It is, however, slow and not now regarded as the best way in which to teach rolling. One puts the paddle across to one side and, sitting curled up forwards, does a straight downward press on the shaft thus coming up if the thrust is quick enough.

HAND ROLL

It is possible to roll a kayak using really skilled technique. No paddle is necessary. One begins with a baths teaching float or a table tennis bat, holding it with both hands angled as for a Steyr roll, and rolls. I have tried to teach people to do it, but, as they have to be very skilful before attempting it, self teaching seems to be the thing with the partner simply acting as a ready prop.

STUNTS

All kinds of stunts may be practised: the clock roll where one spins the kayak around and around on the surface by repeatedly switching hand grip on the submerged shaft and then rolling up; or the dry hat, cigarette or cup of tea stunt where one holds the object in the hand and capsizes, passing the item across the up-turned hull of the canoe into the other hand and then rolling up using the put across roll. Some people can sit in a canoe, capsize it, swim to the other end of the baths hanging upside down, head down and then hand roll up.

Chapter 8

Reading Rivers

Musicians will read music at sight and play it correctly. There may be slight differences in accent in each performance but the basic sound remains as the score directs. So it is with canoeing. The skilled canoeist reads the water and moves accordingly imposing his own style on the pattern of movements. Most of the basic movement patterns have already been explained. This section sets out to point out the clues that the water provides—the finer points of detail on the sheet of music that make all the difference between pedestrian plonking and inspired enjoyment.

The first and most important lesson that one learns about water is that it has weight. One cubic foot of water weighs about 62 lb. and the average canoe will contain about 12 to 14 cu. ft. of water when waterlogged. A waterlogged canoe can weigh as much as half a ton and if that weight is moving at about 4 or 5 m.p.h. an impact with a solid object will very likely crush the canoe.

Mainstream

Imagine a river with a rectangular cross section of even depth right across the bed. In no place is it less deep than in any other. It is easy to see that the water will move uniformly from the higher end of the river to the lower end, its speed will be the same right across the river, and it will all be moving the same way. If the river has infinite depth the flow of water will not be impeded by interaction with the bottom, because there isn't one. If the river is so shallow that at some stage the bottom reaches the top level of the water, then we have a damp flat surface and the water does not move at all. Somewhere between the very deep river and the very shallow river there will be a time when the surface movement of the water will begin to be affected by the decreasing depth of the water. The critical depth when the stream 'feels bottom' is dependent on the velocity of the river.

A normal river has shallow sections, deep sections, obstacles and smooth parts. All these conditions may be found in crossing one part of the river. The surface flow of the water must, therefore, move with varying speed. So far theory leads us to assume that the water all moves in the same direction with varying speeds. In fact, because of the ability of water to turn corners quite sharply, and thus form eddies, some parts of the river will be moving contrary to the usual direction of the river. Eddy currents are found behind rocks and at the side of fast moving spouts of water which enter slow moving water.

The first rule of reading the water is, *When moving with the river seek the mainstream; when moving against the river avoid the mainstream and seek the eddies.*

Identifying the mainstream is a skill which grows with practice. The mainstream will always

1. Seek the deepest part of the river.
2. Take the outside of a bend.
3. Kick up the biggest turbulence when reaching the still water.
4. Move fastest in the direction of the river.
5. Give more chances to roll if in difficulties.
6. Offer the most violent changes of velocity thus causing capsizes.

Before attempting a rapid section which seems difficult, walk along the banks and identify the run of the mainstream through the rocks and over the shallows. The International River Grading Scale indicates that most people will read the Grade 1 and 2 rivers fairly easily, but Grade 3 becomes difficult and interesting and Grade 4 makes demands on previous experience and skill in judging water flows and where the obstacles are. Grades 5 and 6 are extremely difficult.

Eddies

The stream will swirl in behind obstacles and cause eddies which move contrary to the general run of the stream. A river extrance, as at Tynemouth, has groynes or short jetties out into the stream to protect the banks and wharfs. Behind these groynes there are swift sharp swirling eddies of water which run almost as fast as the main current but in the opposite direction. By the accidental discovery of these when in a race competing against K1 canoes and other racing craft, whilst using a slalom canoe, slow by racing standards, I came in third overall beating nearly all the racing canoes having regained half a mile of lost distance in one mile. The racing canoes were stemming a racing flood tide sweeping in between the river banks, and I was nipping smartly around the sharp corners at the ends of the groynes, meeting the racing tide only briefly about every hundred yards.

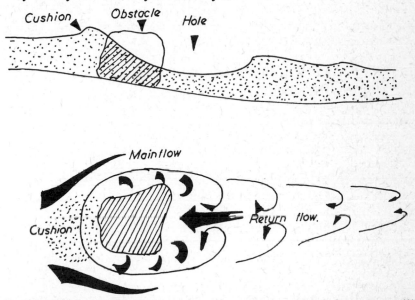

Coming downstream one may see a rock ahead and the water will be heaped up in front of it—a water cushion which pushes floating objects to one side or the other before they can strike the rock. Immediately behind the rock the water swirls round into a depression. If the canoe is paddled up in the tail from the rock it is easy suddenly to pick up speed a few feet from the rock and find a smart collision inevitable.

The rock trails a tail of eddying water for some distance behind it, running downstream of course. It is possible to paddle up a rapid by using the tails from various rocks as steps to assist progress against the current. However, there will always be a 'crux', usually at the top of the rapid, where the water sweeps over in a smooth stream of considerable force and velocity. It may not be possible to find a tail of eddies just here and sheer sprint power may not be enough. Expert canoeists are not very often to be found racing down rapid after rapid but they are often to be found playing about with a fast moving rapid trying to go up it.

The skill that the canoeist in the rapid is developing is that of reading eddy currents and of learning how to handle them. It should be noted that eddies are found rotating in horizontal, transverse and vertical planes. The horizontal eddy is found behind exposed rocks and at the side of spouts; the vertical eddy is found below weirs and large rocks over which the water flows.

Eddy currents are to be found:

1. Behind exposed obstacles.
2. Behind hidden obstacles.
3. Where a fast moving stream enters a still area of water.
4. Toward the inside of a bend where the mainstream runs outside.
5. Rotating in a horizontal plane, usually behind exposed obstacles.
6. Rotating in a vertical plane behind covered obstacles like weirs.
7. Rotating in both planes as with a large rock partly submerged and surrounded by fast running spouts of water. The 'Cauldron' on the river Leven at high water is such a place.
8. Rotating along an axis in line with the river flow. These are sometimes called "corkscrews."

Whirlpool

Eddies will form whirlpools if the conditions are right. Look out for a whirlpool in a river which is wider than average at some point, where the fast moving water is offset to one side and the backwater is wide and deep. The 'eye' of the whirlpool will move about around a centre. These eddies are not violent affairs such as the 'Maelstrom' is reputed to be nor will whole canoes vanish from sight within them. One may paddle across them with no more difficulty than a sudden shift of balance as the eye is crossed. It is when the swimmer is mixed up within the rotating current that serious trouble will be experienced unless a simple drill is followed.

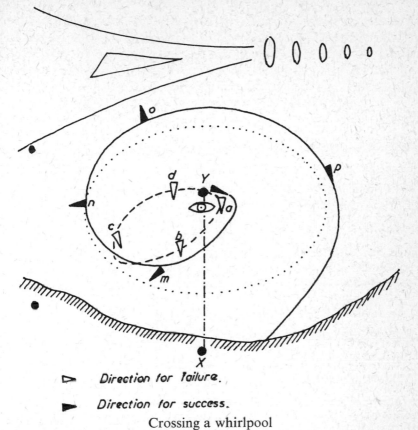

▷   *Direction for failure.*

▶   *Direction for success.*

Crossing a whirlpool

Suppose that the pool rotates at a speed of about $1\frac{1}{2}$ m.p.h. and that the swimmer towing his canoe swims at 1 m.p.h. in the direction Y—X. He sets out in that direction but is swept upstream by the flow at B. He turns to face the point X and at point C is battling into a $1\frac{1}{2}$ m.p.h. current which sweeps him around the bend. Because of his angled attack to the water flow he in fact ferry glides back toward the centre of the pool. At D he is making progress back toward the eye and feels his progress to be accelerating and therefore satisfactory. At A he is moving toward X with maximum velocity but such is his speed that he spends very little time there and distance over the ground toward his objective is minimal. Eventually he continues to trace out an elliptical orbit, the major axis of which is angled toward X and upstream of it.

After two or three rotations a sense of helplessness sets in.
The proper way in which to tackle whirlpools as a swimmer is to
swim away from the eye of the whirl until free from the pull of the
current. At Y one swims in the direction of the black arrow. At M
the eye of the pool is directly behind and the aim is upstream of X.
At N the direction is directly upstream and the eye of the pool is
directly behind the swimmer. At O the swimmer is heading
directly away from X and by now is well out of the centre of the
whirl. At P the pull of the whirl is so slight that he may now start
to follow a curving path in towards the point of landing, probably
slightly downstream of X.

Spouts

An evenly running sheet of water moving swiftly is no great
problem, but if the speed of the surface varies from place to place
because of obstacles then it becomes difficult to run the section.
The simplest form of this problem is where a fast moving spout
of water sweeps down into an area of relatively still water. This

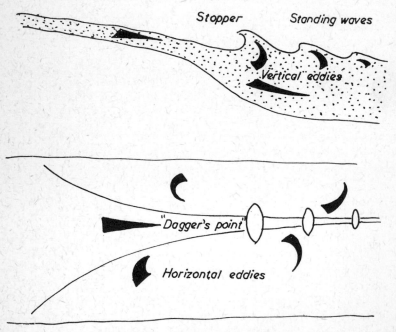

Vertical and horizontal eddies

Mike Ramsay at Hambledon, producing the action that won for Stew Frazer (the photographer) the award for the sports photograph of the year at the Hague in 1967. This is a deliberate loop, under full control the whole way. Water moving left to right, 8 mph. Surfing leads to such mastery. A full day's continuous work in winter conditions and several reels of film went into obtaining this remarkable photograph.

L.C.4

will occur where shallows give place to deep water. Horizontal eddies are found at either side of the spout and vertical eddies in the spout where it strikes the deep water.

The proper way in which to gain experience in tackling water spouts is to find a good simple one with a large long pool after it so that a capsize will leave one time to reach the side to avoid being swept over the next rapid. The skills of break-in and break-out in the tail of the spout are learned first. If the spout is particularly powerful, as with the Thames weirs, then vertical eddies will be very strong and it is necessary to start well down the spout and move higher up toward the source of the spout as skill grows. Note that deep water rescue techniques are very often the best way of dealing with a capsize (if rolling is not possible) on the large rivers. Sometimes exit along the banks is very difficult.

Having learned to handle the horizontal eddies, go on to the vertical eddies by first learning to roll. Then ride the face of the standing waves, or haystacks, as the vertical eddies are called. A mistake here may mean a capsize and roll but really fierce haystacks, especially the first which is called the stopper, may loop the canoe. Looping is fun but only if it's done deliberately. The vertical eddy is usually the most difficult to handle. Once skill below the rapid is gained it is possible to run the rapid from above and to know that one may pull out into safety in a chosen place. If you are not sure of this choose a little eddy at the side behind a specified rock and see if you can swing the bows of the canoe into the 'slot' followed by the rest of the canoe without losing station. It is surprising how often one starts turning and manages to latch in to another slot about 30 yards downstream, missing the selected place by a long way.

Stopper wave

The most startling of the vertical eddies is the stopper, which is the first wave one meets when going down the spout. Little ones, as on Grade 2 rapids, are not bad but the Grade 4 stopper stops the canoe. The effect is as if one were in a sports car moving rapidly, when the brakes are applied very forcibly. It is possible to be slammed through the footrest if it is weak, so that the front of the cockpit cuts across one's stomach. Properly equipped canoes now avoid this damage and difficulty but the jerk of a sudden stop is

Monschau: a C2 breaking out of the fast moving water (left to right) to enter the gate. The counter leaning bodies balance each other, the bow man thrusts all his paddle deep into the water to obtain maximum possible bite . . . the top surface is largely air, so solid water must be found deep down. The stern of this canoe is moving left to right at about ten mph., the bows right to left at about two mph., and the resultant spin is violent and the strain on the canoe structure is enormous. The men must be locked into position in the canoe with knee braces, thigh straps, and foot bars to prevent their being hurled out. In a capsize the experts must roll, because to release the strappings in the ten to twenty seconds that most people can manage under water whilst their heads are being banged off the rocks over which they are rushing at between five and ten mph., is too difficult.

quite severe. It is essential to keep on paddling through these waves. There is a distinct feeling of horror on meeting one's first real stopper because it appears to hover overhead, and then the temptation to stop paddling and hold the paddle high is very strong. Resist, and paddle as if your life depended on it. In fact it might, and canoes have been swallowed by stoppers and then spat out in pieces.

Really big stoppers are best avoided by taking to the edge, but taking care not to move over into the curling eddies which then pull one out to the side. There is usually a narrow band of possible water between the Scylla of the stopper and the Charybdis of the contrary eddies.

One may play with the stopper by performing the high cross across the spout on the upstream face of the stopper, the canoe surfing across from one side to the other. When breaking in to the spout at this high speed point balance must be perfect and on really big stoppers it is possible to be too slow and be sucked down sideways into the stopper; or dive in too fast forwards and loop out backwards over the stopper.

High cross: Body ahead of crest.

Weir slot

I use this term for want of a better one. The weir presents a level obstacle to the water flow which sweeps over it in a straight line and curls back in a stopper of some length. Natural stoppers tend to be single humps of water just on a spout but weir stoppers present a long line of returning water tumbling over and over. The weir stopper may not be very high but it may be of considerable extent and will return floating obstacles for some distance. The onward flowing water is deep down under the returning stopper.

Between the downward sweep of the water from the weir and the downward sweep of the returning stopper, there is a clear slot with a wall on each side. There are four ways out of this watery trench—over the stopper, which is usually impossible if it is more

Expression of grim determination. A racing canoe on the Liffey Descent in Ireland, now an international event ranking with the Sella River race in Spain. Big firms are beginning to sponsor more and more canoeing events in Britain and all over Europe. This is a weir slot, a most unpleasant place to be.

than 3 or 4 in. high, under the stopper, which is impossible if one is wearing a lifejacket which lifts one up into the returning water too quickly, preventing escape downstream, or out at either end. It is possible either to use a hanging support or draw stroke onto the stopper side of the slot, angling the blade to move either to one end of the slot or to the other depending on which angle is used. If one is very skilful, it is possible to paddle forward in the normal way, taking great care to put no weight on the blade on the weir side lest it be swept under the canoe and the whole lot turned over causing one's helmeted(?) head to be slammed against the weir cill. This is usually quite shallow—about 6 to 12 in. deep just under the downflow. It is possible when out of the canoe momentarily to put one's feet down on the cill, crouch and spring and plunge headlong over the stopper and so out to safety.

Stopper loop

Weirs are usually regarded as dangerous. It is easy to go over a weir, in fact, but it is a clever canoeist who can control events in the turbulence below the weir. It is essential to keep the canoe at right angles to the weir when passing through the stopper, or it will swing sideways and whilst one may balance the canoe in the slot for some time, it becomes very confusing to be held in the slot trying to think of a way out. The water thunders down about one's ears, the canoe bucks and kicks, a paddle blade may be smashed off on the weir cill as neatly as with a pair of shears. The big brace over the stopper edge may not be strong enough, in which case edge along to the ends. If you bale out the canoe may be smashed to little pieces.

In order to learn how to handle a weir slot learn the big brace and the hanging draw stroke and then find a tiny little weir stopper, or long stopper, over a natural ledge of rock with a vertical depth of less than 4 in. Practise running the length of the slot from end

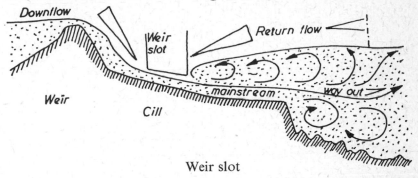

Weir slot

to end and have safety men stationed ready to pick up the bits. The river Tees, for example, presents many such places where it pours over the slabs of the whinstone cill.

Interaction, hull-water

A moving hull in water will create divergent bow and stern waves in addition to lateral stern waves. The bow wave exists in depth as well as sideways. In shallow water the downward, diverging, bow wave will strike bottom and the wave effect will be returned towards the stern of the canoe and affect it. In deep water the effect is negligible. As one enters shallow water the bows sit up, the stern squats and the following stern wave closes up and starts to hiss; at the same time paddling becomes very difficult and the water feels viscous and heavy. Provided the power stroke is maintained the attempt by the canoe to climb onto the plane will maintain the bow-up attitude. If now one eases the power stroke the stern wave catches up, lifting the stern and depressing the bow;

Rising bows   Squatting stern

Bottom drag
Interaction, hull-water

this is akin to surfing on one's own stern wave and the canoe
broaches to run sideways on it.

The novice will find that if he enters shallow water the bows
climb and the stroke becomes difficult so he eases the stroke. The
bows then dip causing the canoe to swing and set off sideways.
When this is repeated confidence is lost. Correction tends to be a
series of backpaddling strokes which continually apply the brakes;
one should of course use a powerful sweep turn to correct the
swing. Spasmodic backpaddling requires constant accelerations
followed by constant decelerations which is extremely tiring.
Cultivate a steady paddling action, keep out of bottom drag and
correct swerves with forward sweep turns on the side to which the
swerve is taking place.

Stern waves from a canoe can cause other canoes to be pulled
inward into its wake. Following another canoe very close by
sitting on its stern wave is called wash-hanging and transfers much
of the effort required for forward travel from the rear to the front
paddler. It is illegal in racing but helpful sometimes in touring
conditions.

Wake riding

Wash-hanging a large boat, call it wake riding, can be great fun
on a river or behind a lake steamer but do not approach from in
front or go within the area shaded in the drawing on page 106.
The screw pulls water from the sides of the hull for some distance
forward of the screw. It is possible to be flung violently under the
counter of a big boat in such circumstances. The first lateral stern
wave is potentially dangerous because there is nothing between
the canoe and the screw and rudder gear. One should aim for the
second wave back. Approach should be on a converging diagonal

K 2's. A sprint start in a long distance canoeing race. The first boat into the lead avoids the churned up surface which is difficult to ride in a 'kicking' boat. Tactics come into this—a leading boat can ease gently over to one side, thus putting the next K boat off course slightly, and with any luck at all the bankside boats will, in addition to coping with bottom drag and paddle blades bouncing off the bottom, be caused to stop or to ram the bank in avoiding the chain re-action thus set up. One or two less to figure at the finish.

from forwards about 30 deg. to the line of travel of the boat.

Do not, for the sake of canoeing's good name and the peace of mind of the masters, go within a hundred yards of 200,000-ton tankers. Disasters do not always strike others and not oneself. If you must go wake riding, do so with some knowledge of the problems involved.

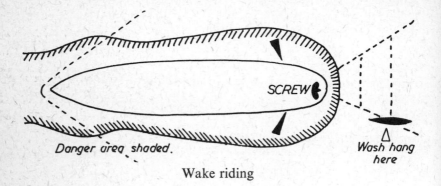

Wake riding

RULE OF THE ROAD

There are many rules of the road. I suggest the following for canoeists.

1. Keep to the right. (There are exceptions.)
2. Keep out of shipping channels if possible. Learn the buoyage systems.
3. Keep out of the way of everything else—for instant acceleration little can match the canoe.
4. Keep a sharp look-out all round.

Chapter 9

River Techniques

Rivers present the basic problem of water moving over a fixed bed. The canoeist on the surface orientates himself with the sides of the river which are linked to the fixed bed and only begins to allow for the strength and direction of movement of the water in all three planes after disasters and difficulties. Having appreciated that water will move in certain ways, it becomes possible to devise methods to deal with basic situations.

FERRY GLIDE

Principle

The canoe is always subject to the influence of the moving water. When moving from one place to another allowance must be made for the continuing water movement. The amount of movement is related to the time during which the flow operates and the speed with which it moves. A knowledge of the Laws of Motion is useful, in fact canoeing would seem to supply situations where these Laws could be given real meaning for students at school or college.

Imagine a smoothly flowing stream running at about 3 m.p.h. with two markers on opposite banks and that one wishes to move along an imaginary line drawn between them. One may move from left to right or right to left, either facing the oncoming stream or facing the opposite way. There are four basic ferry glides: forward left, forward right, reverse left and reverse right.

Forward right ferry glide

1. The canoe is pointing upstream.
2. The river is flowing past the right shoulder.

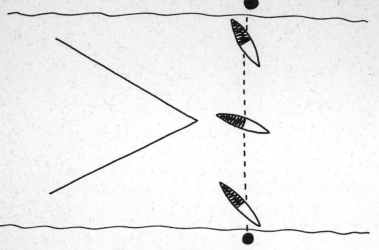

Forward right ferry glide

3. Swing the bows out to the right about 45 deg. to the stream line.
4. Paddle forward steadily.
5. The canoe moves out into the stream.
6. As the canoe moves into faster water it is necessary to prevent the current swinging the bows downstream.
7. To prevent a downstream move, either
    (a) Paddle harder, or
    (b) Turn upstream at a sharper angle, or
    (c) Paddle on the downstream side only.
8. As the canoe spans the fast moving stream the turn will cease but a downstream drift will develop if,
    (a) One backpaddles on whatever side for whatever reason,
    (b) The action is not sufficiently powerful,
    (c) The bows of the canoe are not angled upstream sufficiently.
9. As the canoe moves out of the fast moving mainstream into the slower boundary currents the canoe will tend to turn upstream.
10. To prevent this,
    (a) Turn the bows more across the stream, more directly towards the mark on the opposite bank,
    (b) Paddle less strongly,

(c) Paddle on the upstream side only.

11. A final hint:
  (a) When leaving slow water for a fast stream lean towards the downstream side.
  (b) When on smooth slow water or smooth fast water, sit upright.
  (c) When moving out of a fast stream into slow water lean towards the upstream side.

Using stream to turn canoe

In ferry glides, especially during practice sessions, it is a good idea to alternate forward and reverse moves, so that it is necessary to turn the canoe completely round during each change from a forward to a reverse ferry glide. The water at the side of the river will be moving slowly, or may even be in a contra-flowing eddy. That is a problem you must deal with from first principles! If a canoe is placed across a stream with one end in fast moving water and the other end in slow water, as at the edge of a spout just after it leaves the constriction which forms it and before it is dissipated in eddy currents, it is possible, by placing the centre of gravity over the boundary layer, to turn the canoe without any paddling effort, apart from balancing strokes, by using the leverage that the stream exerts on the hull.

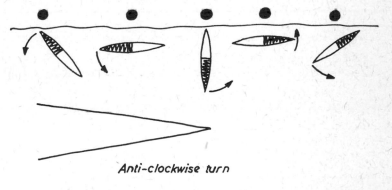

Anti-clockwise turn

Points to note:
  1. The canoe may turn clockwise or anti-clockwise (viewed from above).

2. If the canoe is facing upstream with the river flowing past the left shoulder the turn should be anti-clockwise.

3. If the canoe is facing upstream with the river flowing past the right shoulder the turn should be clockwise.

4. If the canoe is facing downstream with the current flowing past the left shoulder the turn should be clockwise.

5. If the canoe is facing downstream with the current flowing past the right shoulder the turn should be anti-clockwise.

6. If there is a grassy bank, a ledge of rock or a pebbly shallows a faster rate of turn is obtained by helping the end of the canoe nearest to it to nudge it or wedge against it. Only GRP canoes will stand that treatment. This applies when the stream or boundary layer is close to the bank.

7. When turning as in 2 above lean to the left.

8. When turning as in 3 above lean to the right.

9. When turning as in 4 above lean to the left.

10. When turning as in 5 above lean to the right.

11. An examiner is usually looking for the candidate's first paddle stroke after he turns from a forward ferry glide to a reverse ferry glide. If it is the correct one to obtain the turns described above the candidate is unlikely to fail.

12. Failure to turn the right way round will result in the canoe scraping along the bank side—rocks, pebbles, low branches and all—as the current takes charge and the canoe moves off downstream. Try a wrong turn in a safe place first to find out.

13. Failure to lean the right way will allow the rotation resulting from the interaction of the fast moving stream across the hull low down and the inertia of the mass of canoeist and canoe higher up, to pass the limits of inherent stability and the canoe will overturn. The natural re-action is a smart slap support stroke on the water on the upstream side, whereupon the stream rushes up the outflung blade driving it down and under the canoe much to the amusement of the watchers and the annoyance or alarm of the canoeist. Fast moving water implies shallow water and that means that the head may strike the bottom. Wear a helmet.

Waltzing

A useful practice on rivers and on surfing waves is 'waltzing' where the canoe is spun around and around by vigorous paddling and balancing action at the edge of a very fast moving spout. Forward and reverse paddling strokes should alternate, otherwise the canoe moves into or out of the stream, losing the turning effect obtained by straddling the boundary eddies. Note that the balance is shifting from side to side as rapidly as the canoe spins and the emphasis is on clear thinking and swift accurate action. In order to learn this, find a spout and practise where it is just about dissipated in eddies and whorls and, as confidence grows, move higher up the spout into the clearly defined barrier area and faster water. This is a natural development of the turning moves previously described.

'S' turn

This is used on a fast moving spout high up and near to its origins The intention is to move to the other side of the spout and, being either too lazy or without sufficient ability to hold the canoe in it. sudden leap from the slow to fast water in a proper ferry glide attitude, one breaks into the stream, accelerates rapidly whilst crossing it, and then breaks out on the other side. This exercise could follow the 'waltzing' move just described by using a half turn one way and a half turn the other way, but across the stream.

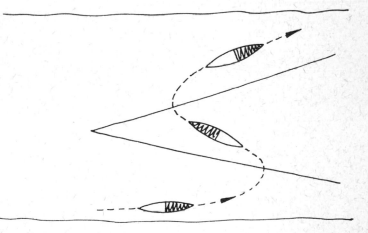

"S" turn

John Woodhouse, Chester Canoe Club, on the River Tay at Grantully. Holes in helmet allow entrapped water to drain out on rising from roll. He is concentrating on entering a 'stopper' and is riding the rising thrust of the water on the flattened left blade. Water is rushing from left to right. Always present bottom of canoe to impinging water flow.

Break-in and break-out (or cut-in and cut-out)

When setting off onto a fast moving river, it is better to start facing upstream so that one may see what obstacles are there; experienced and confident paddlers will perhaps set off backwards, with stern to stream, if it suits their purpose. At Proficiency Certificate level it is better to set off facing upstream.

Left forward break-in

1. Face upstream with the stream passing on the left.
2. Left bow rudder.
3. As the bows enter the stream, lean left.

4. Swing into a high telemark.
5. Regain balance and set off downstream in the centre of the fast moving water.

Right forward break-in

1. Face upstream with the stream passing on the right.
2. Right bow rudder.
3. As the bows enter the stream, lean right.
4. Swing into a high telemark.
5. As before.

Right reverse break-in

1. Face downstream with the stream passing the right shoulder.
2. Right stern 'bow' rudder (or reverse stern rudder).
3. As the stern breaks into the stream swing into a hanging draw position (or reverse high telemark).
4. Lean right.
5. As before.

Left reverse break-in

1. Face downstream with the stream passing on left.
2. Left reverse stern rudder.
3. As the stern enters fast moving water, lean left.
4. Swing into a reverse high telemark.
5. As before.

Left forward break-out

1. Paddle fast downstream, facing forwards.
2. Move towards left edge of fast moving water and select a still place at the side.
3. Aim at the bank at a point some way upstream of the place where the break-out is to finish.
4. As the canoe is angled across the fast water and the bows enter the still water, say 20 ft. upstream of the exit point, use a left high telemark, blade in still water at side. It may be necessary to use a right forward sweep stroke to put the canoe where a left high telemark may be used.
5. Lean well over to the left.
6. Push the bows of the canoe into the bank by driving hard with the left paddle when balance is regained after the telemark. If the spin is not stopped rotational momentum may carry the

bows back into the fast moving water and an uncontrolled break-out may possibly result.

7. The canoe is now facing upstream with the bows nudging the selected rock or clump of grass. (This takes a great deal of practice and judgment.)

8. Practise the three other break-out moves.

High cross

The exercises with the fast moving spout of water will develop an ability to ride the sudden rotational accelerations around both the

River Leiser at Spittal: International course. C2 tackling grade four to five water. Note rescue man with wet suit and waist line high on right, and rescue rubber dinghy high centre right. 15 R indicates the fifteenth gate in sequence, to be taken in reverse from this side. 16 is a downstream forward gate. 14 is a forward upstream gate. Canoe must break out right immediately after gate 13 and swing upstream into 14. The trap here is to be swept through gate 15 R before being able to attempt 14. How would you tackle this sequence? There are many ways.

vertical central axis and the longitudinal axis. The high cross, if carried out on really fast water as at a weir outfall, may result in a loop which is a complete rotation about the lateral axis. The high cross may only take place where there is a sizeable stopper wave at the bottom of a fast moving spout. By sizeable I mean that the wave should have a crest about three feet plus half the length of the canoe away from the downrunning water which sweeps up into it. It must be possible to shove the canoe over the forward edge of the crest so that the centre of gravity is forward of the crest without the bows digging into the downrunning water.

1. Ensure that no-one is about to shoot the rapid leading to the stopper.
2. Paddle upstream in the relatively still water in the narrowing wedge-shaped area at the side of the spout.
3. Sprint the last few yards and draw stroke the bows into the hollow upstream of the stopper. The body should be just forward of the stopper crest.
4. Lean out onto a powerful high draw to pull the whole canoe onto the face of the wave.
5. When on the face, sit upright and allow a surfing action at a slight angle to the water to move the canoe across the face of the wave.
6. When breaking out into the relatively still water on the other side of the stopper lean the other way on a low telemark with the blade on the face of the stopper wave. The canoe drops off the face with a distinct bounce down.
7. The spout is usually very narrow so the move is very short.
8. The water is usually very fast and the move is quick.
9. One must switch balance through anything up to 180 deg. in a moment.
10. If a mistake is made, use a deep high draw over the crest of the stopper. This may not work and one may find oneself locked onto the stopper in a broached surfing position with the paddle buried deep in the heart of the stopper. Pulling over the crest may not work. Some people recommend rolling with it (i.e. falling over upstream) using the drag of the body in the water to pull one through the crest. See the section on weir slots on page 116.

11. A variation, requiring very quick responses to the twitching of the canoe, is to ride the centre of the stopper crest and remain there. Remember not to hog it thus keeping others off it. Steering is almost entirely by body balance—leaning right to turn left, for example.

12. Too fast an entry from the still water into the pre-stopper hollow may result in a loop. If the water is deep enough to allow the bows to swing under then damage is likely to be minimal, although the deck may crush inwards, momentarily, if not sufficiently stiff.

    Armathwaite weir on the Eden near Penrith is reputed to have smashed five canoes one after the other as the paddlers tried bow loops in rock-studded stoppers. However, GRP canoes are easily stuck together again in the workshop—if recovered.

13. High cross techniques may be picked up on the smaller waves, say two or three back from the initial stopper, until one gets the courage to enter the thrashing, pounding, roaring hole.

Weir slots

The weir slot has been described on page 100. It is really a long, wide, but not very high, stopper. Its power should not be underestimated. There are four ways out of a weir slot: over the top, under the stopper and out at either end. The remote possibility of portaging over the weir may be discounted.

1. Find a little weir slot, so slight that it will only just hold the canoe in the broached position, but will allow one to high draw over it. It should be about 3 in. to 4 in. deep.

2. Paddle into it from one end or over it from the centre. Swing sideways into the broached position.

3. Use a high draw stroke into the stopper crest, not too deep or the canoe will be pulled out over the top. Angle the blade one way as in the hanging draw and wait for the reaction. The moving water spraying off the blade will be deflected to one side of the blade or the other instead of downwards as in a high draw. This reaction will cause the canoe slowly to pick up movement away from where it was when the stroke started. Movement is away from the blade edge which is angled away from the canoe.

4. Try it on faster water.
5. Another method, possible on not very powerful slots, is to paddle along the crest of the stopper by leaning and paddling on the downstream blade.
6. It will usually be found that there is a way out of either end of most stopper or weir slots. Beware of the slot which extends without break from smooth mill wall to smooth retaining wall. There is probably no way out, the only way in being over the top, either the weir edge, or the stopper crest.

Weir slot, no canoe

If one has the misfortune to lose one's canoe in the slot, despite all efforts to get it out, then one will experience oscillation as follows:

1. Into and under the downfalling water from the weir.
2. Driven down, lifejacket and all, under and away from the weir.
3. Lifejacket lifts the body up into the forward edge of the stopper crest.
4. The downcurling water from the stopper crest returns the body to the weir downfall. The oscillation period is about six seconds.

Therefore:

1. If the slot is small try to stand up on the weir cill. Once the weight is on the feet the downrushing water may not be strong enough to sweep them away. Leap over the stopper crest.
2. If the slot is powerful and the end of the slot is near and open try to swim toward it. Turbulence in the water may turn the body around resulting in movement away from safety.
3. If the slot is powerful and there is no open end, or the slot end is a long way off, start to take off the lifejacket. A quick release knot or buckle is essential. Take off the lifejacket and throw it over the stopper crest. Dive deep and stay down as long as possible in the strong downstream underwater current. Look for the lifejacket on the other side and hang on to it.
4. If someone else gets into this difficulty and you are on the bank, tie a line to a lifejacket and throw it or float it over the weir to some place the far side of the man in difficulty; the stopper slot will hold it in. Pull it towards the end of the slot

but only when the man appears momentarily on his return into the slot. When contact is made, reel him in along the slot.

5. Remember that this advice is probably of no use whatever in an emergency but it may start you thinking now so that in the crisis your mind remains cool.

Wash-hanging

One may play about with surfing techniques on rivers even though the nearest stopper may be hundreds of miles away. Wash-hanging other canoes is possible but prohibited in the racing rules. Wash-hanging a boat can be either fun or necessary, depending on the place. Points to watch are as follows:

1. If the boat is wide in the beam, short and heavily loaded, it will probably kick up a good stern wave.
2. If the boat is going much faster than about 6 knots drag may pull one back over the stern wave.
3. Speed boats which have planing hulls and which are efficient when planing but not when going slow will often considerably slow down when passing canoeists which of course kicks up a monster stern wave ideal for wash-hanging if one can catch it. Speed boats on the plane should move quickly past canoeists if they do not wish to shake them up. Most advanced canoeists enjoy a good bouncing on a calm river—it reduces boredom! I suppose it depends on what one is doing.
4. Eventually a steady state will be found where the angle of the canoe, the angle of the wave face and the efficiency of the canoe hull will all balance, and 'free-wheeling' is possible.

Chapter 10

Estuaries and Buoyage

An estuary is neither sea nor river; its nature is quite distinct. It is both river and sea: tidal river and a sea within the river bed. The river mouth is the place where shipping congregates and in which mountains of mud collect and disperse. Through these shifting banks the ships must find their way and man-made marks are essential to assist in this search. A knowledge of the marks and what they mean may be most useful to the canoeist.

Each estuary is quite different from every other estuary. It is necessary to know your own estuary and be prepared to learn again any other estuary. Rivers usually obey certain natural laws and have characteristics which are found in most other rivers; the sea is very complicated and some of its natural difficulties have been mentioned in this book; but the estuary permutates and combines the problems of sea and river into situations of peculiar difficulty.

Mud and sand banks

The river carries with it the mud and fine silt scoured from the land and will carry it so long as the water is in movement. When tide and river flows are in balanced opposition, the silt settles as the water stops its movement and this may take place anywhere along the tidal stretches of a river. Mud is found further from the sea while sand is found closer to the sea. On either side of the waterways there are often mud flats, creeks and marshes; land attractive to wild fowl, hunters and industry alike.

The marshes are threaded with waterways which are tidal and which become thin trickles of muddy water at low tide. These streams cut their ways out across the tidal sands and mud flats, cutting up the low tide mud into quaking bogs surrounded by

119

gravelly sewers containing swallet holes in the bends in the streams.

In some ways this desolation of mud and difficulty is depressing, and yet there is this rare sense of quiet and solitude, keening wind and birds' cries. Try not to hurry in an estuary.

At high tide progress is easy. Launching is no problem from a handy beach, a gravel hard or a jetty. One potters off along the creeks and returns six hours later to a waste of rotting timbers festooned with weed, old anchor flukes hung with flaking chains, and an expanse of mud; all this was hidden under the high tide.

When acres of mud separate one from a landing place test the gravel under the canoe until a firm place is found. This is not easy as the tide will be sluicing about and the ebb, with the power of the river to help it, may be too strong for one to stand.

Step out, sit on the grounded canoe and lace up your plimsolls firmly. Untie the painter and put the paddle in the cockpit. Step out very gingerly; ankle deep mud is quite possible to walk through but calf-deep mud is a little difficult. Be ready for the hole under the mud into which one sinks knee or thigh deep. If this happens, pull the canoe across the mud, over which it will slide very easily, and lie across it whilst pulling your legs out of the sucking mud.

At this point one realises that the only way to tackle mud is to spread the load. A local fisherman lies across the stern of his little dinghy and runs down the mud using his boat as a toboggan, his weight supported by the transom and his feet on short boards scattering mud from the surface.

Pull the canoe across one's front so that the chest lies over the cockpit hole, the face a foot from the mud and the knees and feet trailing lightly on the surface of the mud. Start a sort of frog-like kick and run, skating the hull sideways over the mud at a run. This is extremely exhausting but one does make progress.

Mud is not the only problem. For example, the Mawddach estuary in Wales has a channel which twists and turns so that, occasionally, on the outgoing run at low tide the channel turns back up the estuary in its meandering and veers away from the sea. These changes of direction may be very confusing. It is possible to disbelieve the evidence of one's senses so that one avoids the running stream of the main channel and seeks some side creek which seems to go the right way but eventually peters out into sand flats. This may mean a difficult portage of upwards of a mile in a strong gusting and gritty wind over sands which are sometimes firm, sometimes soft. If you must walk always take the canoe with you—it may be needed to provide a platform onto which one can climb out of the quaking sands. If all else fails sit in the canoe on the sand, eat and drink, and wait. Don't signal for a lifeboat—it may not be able to come closer than the sand bar at the mouth several miles away. A helicopter might lift you out, leaving your canoe and its gear to the mercy of the incoming tide. Be patient and never hurry in an estuary.

THE MAIN CHANNEL

The main channel is the cleared, dredged channel, along which the ships pass. This channel is buoyed and these great floating obstacles may perform some very odd gyrations in the sluicing tide.

Some points to note are as follows:

1. Left and right of channel are calculated as one enters the estuary from the sea.
2. Left marks, called can buoys, are red, or red and white, and flat topped.
3. Right marks, called conical buoys, are black, or black and white, and conical topped.
4. Centre marks, indicating a divided channel, are spherical.
5. Wreck buoys are green, or green and white, and labelled 'Wreck'.
6. Side turns into offshoot creeks are marked with tall poles and small floats, may be orange or yellow; these may be confused with mooring floats, of course.
7. Ships move without a great deal of engine noise and when downwind from a group of canoeists their arrival may not be heard until the rush of the bow wave is almost overhead. Of course the ship will have been blowing its siren for some time but in a shipping channel all the various hoots and toots sound much the same to the non-expert. However, remember that five or more short blasts on a siren indicate that a pilot is in doubt, of which you may be the cause.

8. Ships move much more quickly than would seem to be possible and stopping them may take several miles.

9. Main channels turn sharply at times and big ships, when turning, go sideways for some distance before settling down, rather like a car skidding in snow. The bow wave of a skidding ship is along its side and, whilst it may be possible to dodge a ship coming head on by paddling very quickly for about fifty feet at right angles to its course, in order to avoid keel-hauling under a skidding ship it may be necessary to sprint for 500 ft. to clear its length. A typical 'skidding' channel is the south-east entrance to Southampton Water as the big ships come in and turn around the Brambles bank.

10. In a sluicing tide a buoy will tug and swing about on the end of its mooring chain, carving out a zigzag wake on the racing water. Such a buoy is the black conical Number 9 off Caernarvon which I like to think of as a vast Welsh witch wearing her pointed hat and swaying from side to side in the tide.

11. Moored buoys lie over in the water and give a clue as to the strength and direction of the tidal flow. As the water rushes by it piles up in front and the effect of 'shooting' a buoy bow wave is like shooting a large and powerful weir on the river. Look out for side-swipes.

12. An excellent little book on estuaries and coastal navigation is *Coastwise Navigation, Notes for Yachtsmen* by G. G. Watkins, Kandy Publications. Reed's *Nautical Almanak*, annually, contains a wealth of information.

13. Keep out of buoyed channels if at all possible.

Other estuary marks

An estuary at night is a very different place.
Some of the points to look for are as follows:

1. Leading lights. As a ship makes landfall and finds the entrance to an estuary, the line on which it should steer is marked by a light standing high a mile or two inland. Closer to the ship and by the water's edge will be another light. The lights will have certain characteristics which make them recognisable. The ship will steer towards the lower light; if the lower light is to the left of the upper light the ship will steer left until the top light

is directly above the lower light, and then the ship is on course. It is quite interesting to try and pick out the leading lights in daylight.

2. There are many kinds of buoys apart from the channel markers; some whistle, hoot, grunt or clang. Others wink red eyes and grumble in their chains.

3. There are many long poles and mooring posts in some rivers, such as the Hamble. It could be quite dangerous to be caught between the hull of a boat and its mooring post as it swings and sways in the tide.

4. The lanes between lines of moored boats present hazards for the canoeist. As he threads his way between the boats, maybe playing hide and seek with the rest of the group, he may suddenly emerge under the bows of a big boat cruising up to its moorings. Such larking about has its dangers.

5. Oil refineries have huge towers laced with light and flares which bloom and shrivel on the wind. The skyline that Fawley presents from Calshot Spit is really quite memorable.

6. Salt flats may lie at the sides of the estuaries. In the dark the romance and mystery of the estuary is most powerful.

Not all estuaries are the busy commercial kind. Most of them are natural and wild with no dredged channel and little to disturb the quiet and calm—except the occasional storms. River and sea have their charms and challenges but the estuary is a place for thought rather than technique.

Chapter 11

Reading Sea Waves

A study of weather will lead one to a better understanding of the nature of waves and their formation. The movement of the water is caused by movement of air which in turn is caused by the formative influences of the weather. This section, however, does not deal with the causes of air movement but concentrates on an attempt to classify wave formations as they affect the canoeist.

The man who receives the black eye is as responsible for it as the man who swings the fist which causes it; in other words, there cannot be an impact unless an object resists a force.

Consider the surface of the sea, or any water for that matter; it is a boundary between water and air, and where it meets the shore all three elements meet: land, sea and air. Theory would lead one to expect (and experience leaves one knowing it) that the shore is where the violence of the energy of moving water and air is most felt.

Slopes on land are easily seen and assessed. A steep uphill road, with a gradient steeper than one in ten will cause most cyclists to dismount, but a motorist in a powerful car with an engine turning at maximum torque will sail up the hill as if it were not there. The cyclist will call the hill steep but the motorist will hardly notice it.

Slopes on the sea are also seen quite easily. The wave is seen and its steepness assessed. But it is difficult to imagine the vast heap of ocean tide as it swells up over the horizon and rises at its peak perhaps twenty feet above its lowest point. Drop a stone into a still pond and the ripples spread outwards. Similarly a low pressure area over the North Sea, causes vast 'ripples' to spread across the sea. Strong winds blowing onshore will also heap up the water on the beach and cause a higher 'tide'. The influences at work on the sea are much more complicated than that of wind only, and wave shapes are not only the small, easily seen, ones. However, this section deals with the easily seen wave forms or their results, as in surfing or tide effects.

The air has slopes—high waves of air with associated troughs; and as air is relatively invisible it is not possible to see and assess these waves without the help of the weather men and their pressure maps. The slope of a hill on land is represented by contours, that on a weather map by isobars; in each case the steepness of the slope is represented by the closeness of the adjacent lines. Imagine a great heap of air, a wave, sixty miles high sweeping across the land at speeds varying from a zephyr to a gale; one may guess at the likely effects by looking at the weather map each night on television, and seeing if the isobars are far apart (calm airs) or close together (wild winds).

The canoeist who goes afloat with no thought for air, water and land, and the shore where they all meet, with no thought for the slopes of the land, the water or the air, may be putting out into danger for himself and for others who have to come to save him.

TERMINOLOGY

Amplitude. The amplitude of a wave is its height measured vertically from the bottom of the trough to the top of the crest.

Wavelength. The wavelength is measured from the crest of one wave to the crest of the next wave in succession.

Frequency. Waves pass a given point at a given rate. The time between a wave crest passing and the next wave crest arriving at a given point is called the period.

Critical depth. A wave 'feels bottom' when it moves into shallow water and begins to break. It will feel bottom before it breaks, so the wave form will be distorted before the actual curling over of the crest begins. The depth at which the break takes place is related to the wavelength and the amplitude and may be called the critical depth. Waves will break when their height is about two-thirds of the depth of the water.

Tide. The twice daily rise and fall of the sea level at any point.

Tide race. The flow of water through, round or over a restriction as a result of the rise and fall of the tide. Most races are reversible depending on the state of the tide.

Tide flood. The tide is flooding when it is rising.

Tide ebb. The tide is ebbing when it is falling.

Spring tide. A time of high high tides and low low tides giving a maximum change of level.

Neap tide. A time of high low tides and low high tides giving a minimum change of level.

Half tide. When the tide is halfway between the top and the bottom of the tide. At this point the rate of change of level of the water is greatest and spring tides will give rise to races of maximum speed. Neap tides will give rise to races of minimum speed.

Slack water. The water is said to be slack when the influence of the tidal movement is minimal. At the top of the tide the water will be slack and also at the bottom of the tide. Spring tides will give rise to short slack periods of half an hour or even less. Neap tides will give long slack periods when otherwise difficult crossings may be attempted when the race is not running.

Dwell. Sometimes, as at Calshot Spit, Southampton, a double effect of the tide is found because the Solent, like an organ pipe, has a resonance which affects the rising tide making it 'dwell' at a certain time in the tide before rising again a little more.

Lee shore and windward shore. A boat is travelling between two shores, and the wind is blowing across the direction of travel of the boat. The side of the boat from which the wind is coming is called the windward, or weather, side of the boat. The shore on that side is called the weather shore, that is, the shore from which the weather is coming. The side of the boat from which the wind is blowing away is called the lee side of the boat, and the shore on that side is called the lee shore.

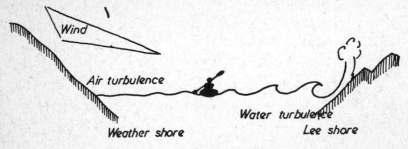

Lee shore and windward shore

A certain confusion tends to exist here, as the observer on the boat sees the weather side of the boat as being the side on which the water is roughest and the lee side of the boat as where the water is calmer, sheltered as it is by the bulk of the boat from the effect of the weather. However, the observer on land sees the weather shore as being the sheltered shore, the bulk of the land keeping the full force of the wind from it; and the lee shore as the worse to be on, the wind having an uninterrupted sweep onto it and bigger and more forceful waves.

Briefly, the weather shore is the sheltered shore and the lee shore is rough.

Fetch. This is the distance that the wave travels from the influence which causes it. The fetch in the definition above is measured from where one is to the weather shore. Just off the weather shore the fetch is small, whilst on the North Sea coast experiencing a north easterly gale the fetch may be the greater part of a thousand miles. The shorter the fetch the less opportunity has the wind to build up long powerful waves.

Overfall. Most cliffs or headlands are the result of resistant rock standing up to the force of the waves. It is a fairly safe bet that in a line with the headland there will be a reef of rock under the surface, pointing out to sea. The water required for the rising of the tide sweeps along the coastline and pours over the

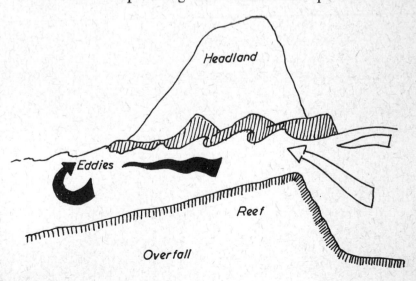

submerged reef just off the headlands. The effect is very like a weir at sea and the rise may be several feet. Associated with the change in level will be turbulence and eddies in a vertical rotation, boiling up from below and for some distance on the down-tide side of the overfall. Overfalls are quite dangerous but may be avoided by going further out to sea, well beyond the point where the depth of the reef becomes sufficient to allow the tidal stream to flow over it without serious surface effects.

Narrows. Where the seaway is narrow, as between a high rocky island and a mainland, the tide race will sweep through between one narrowing rock face and another. This may give rise to a venturi effect and severe turbulence with interfering waves causing something like overfalls in the channel. The leading edge of an island is like the bows of a vast ship, setting up a bow wave in a tide race. A headland may also set up similar 'bow' waves. Where these waves meet one finds a series of standing waves as on a river rapid. If a powerful sea wave form is also met in narrows the random effects of doubling waves, interference and turbulence from vertical and horizontal eddies may kick up a hideous sea, as between Bardsey Island and the Lleyn Peninsula.

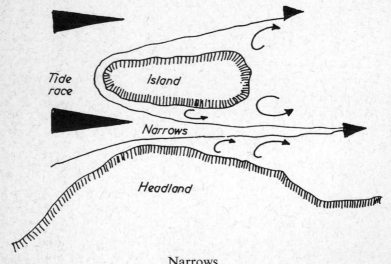

Narrows

Half tide reefs. A half tide reef is one which affects the waves for the lower half of the tidal range but allows most waves to flow uninterrupted over it at high tide. At about half tide the reef will start to cause the waves to break. At Southerndown beach in South Wales, the waves coming up the Bristol Channel must fight the outgoing tide until low water. As the flow begins the tide assists the waves up the channel and they begin to arrive at the beach about half tide. However, about a mile offshore is a reef covered at high tide. The waves dissipate much of their energy against the reef in the lower range of the tide; within a few minutes the tide, which is rising at its maximum rate at half tide, allows the waves to clear the reef without breaking and dissipating their energy. The result is that the beach is quite suddenly subjected to quite large surf after hours of small waves. The change takes about ten to fifteen minutes. Canoeists on a longshore paddle and without surfing experience could be caught unawares and find themselves in serious difficulties.

DEEP WATER WAVES

Wave formation

There are several theories to account for wave formation; I prefer the orbiting particle theory even though the results are faulty and not truly representative of the true shape of waves.

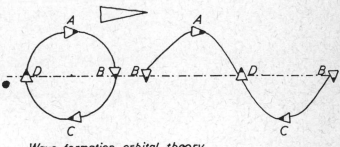

Wave formation, orbital theory.

Orbiting particle theory

A At this point the particle is moving forward under the influence of the wind as part of the crest of the wave. It is here that the wind transfers some of its vast energy to the water and the

L.C.5

longer and harder the wind blows the more energetic will be the resulting waves. The wave shape moves on but the particle is left behind.

B   The particle being left behind by the wave sinks down the back of the wave. Here the water is moving directly downwards and in a canoe, on that part of the wave, one has a distinct sinking feeling.

C   This is the trough, and here the particle is moving backwards contrary to the movement of the wave formation; in a canoe one has a distinct sensation of being swept into the face of the next wave as it approaches.

D   The face of the wave sweeps up towards the crest of the next wave. At 'D' the water particle is moving directly upwards. This is where the lifejacketed swimmer becomes swamped by water if his buoyancy to weight ratio is not enough to give him the necessary upward acceleration to clear the wave crest.

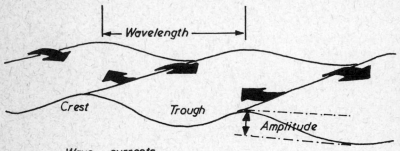

Wave   currents

Wave currents

Each wave has local currents running on its surface, in the direction of the wave in the crest, and in the contrary direction in the trough. A canoeist will feel an acceleration in the trough towards the next crest when paddling into the waves and a slowing down when rising through the crest. Going with the waves the canoeist will be caught and passed by each wave in turn and the crest will help him along. Down in the trough there is a distinct wallowing feeling as the contrary trough current slows down progress.

Taking the waves at an angle, going towards the wave crest will result in the bows swinging away from the arriving crest, and as the crest passes under the canoe the bows will swing towards the next crest. Progress will be made in a series of swerves and the resultant course is somewhere between the two extremes of the swerves. It is necessary to take care when a large wave arrives as, if the angle to the wave of the canoe is too fine, the bows will swing away with the crest and the canoe will swing round pointing at right angles to its proper course.

Apart from the directional instability which the wave currents cause there will be a lateral instability. One should lean into the wave crest, toward the wave as it approaches and as it recedes. It is possible to time the paddle strokes to resist the turning swing of the canoe and to lend stability over the crest. The problem is not so difficult in the trough. It should be remembered also that wind force is greatest in the crest.

WAVES, WIND AND TIDE

Waves with wind

If the waves and the wind are travelling in the same direction, the wave will tend to build up its energy; it will retain its smooth form and will be quite easy to paddle across but the lee shore will have high surf.

Waves against wind

After the waves have been formed and they continue on their way, they will eventually meet a wind which blows against them. This has the effect of making the face of the wave short and steep and, perhaps, break, whilst the back of the wave becomes gently sloped. The wind blowing against the set of the waves will first set up a surface chop, and second take the power out of the original wave form. Wind against wave is a difficult canoeing situation.

Waves against tidal flow

When a sea race begins to move, as off Ramsey Island, South Wales, if it runs against the set of the waves then it will shorten and steepen them. If the waves are running about 8 to 10 knots, and the tide is running about 6 to 7 knots then the waves will actually pass any given point at about 2 to 3 knots, but their frequency will remain the same. This implies a severe shortening of the wave length with an increase in amplitude so great that the waves may break. Breaking waves 10 to 15 ft. high can be found on a day when the surf on the nearby beach is 18 in. high, too small for canoeing fun.

Other variations

It may be seen that tide and wave and wind may be together; or at an angle each to the other; or interfering or assisting wave formation. In any event these three influences spell trouble for canoeists.

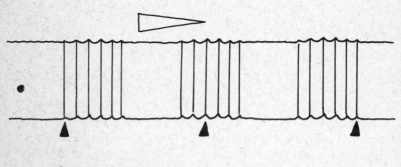

Boxing or grouping waves

Boxing or grouping waves

This effect may best be seen in a short choppy wave formation. Big waves with a long fetch are too big for the effect to be noticed except for the so called 'seventh wave' being bigger than the rest.

In a wave formation travelling in a given direction it may be observed that there are groups of waves, sometimes called boxes of waves, which are clearly larger than those waves either behind or before them. The boxes travel in the same direction as the waves but not so quickly as the waves themselves. The individual wave may be seen to be small but to catch up with the back of a box. It enters the box and gathers amplitude and as it passes through the box it becomes largest about the middle of the box, continuing with its advance until it fades away out of the front of the box, eventually to catch up with the next box and so on.

Just prior to the boxes arriving at the shore there will be surf breaking of small amplitude and with few lines of breaking waves. As the waves of increasing amplitude begin to arrive they break further out and with greater force. When the centre of the box passes the waves begin to decrease in size and force until the next box arrives.

In a canoe it is possible, being quite nervous about entering the breaking waves, to hold off just to the sea side of the break line. One sits there pondering the chances, sees the box diminish, and moves further in to take advantage of the smaller waves but fails to move right in and remains sitting thinking. There then comes a seething roar, the first of the next box is breaking to the seaward side of the canoe and one is right in the break line where the violence of dissipation of the wave's energy is greatest. Horrifying!

Interfering wave forms

A wave formation is moving with a certain amplitude, wave length and frequency in a certain direction. Another wave formation has, for the sake of illustration, the same character exactly. The two wave forms arrive at a certain point, with their crests exactly together (that is, 'in phase'). It is clear that the resulting wave form will have the same wavelength and frequency but double the amplitude of the two basic forms. If the two wave

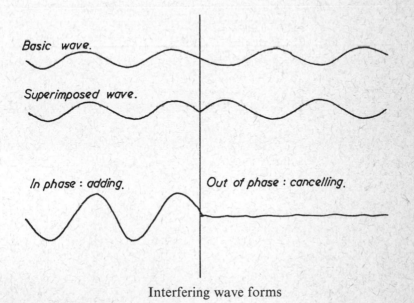

Interfering wave forms

forms arrive at a given place so that the crest of one coincides
with the trough of the other, they will exactly cancel each other
('out of phase') and the resultant wave is flat.

In nature this situation is rarely met. What does happen is that
two or more wave forms, each with its own wavelength, frequency
and amplitude will arrive from different directions at a given
point and the resulting water may be tumbled and rough one
minute and uneasily calm the next.

Crossing waves

Two wave formations of similar character are moving at an angle
one to the other. At any given moment the crest of one wave will
be cutting across the other wave formation, crossing crest and
trough as it travels. The crests of each form add together being in

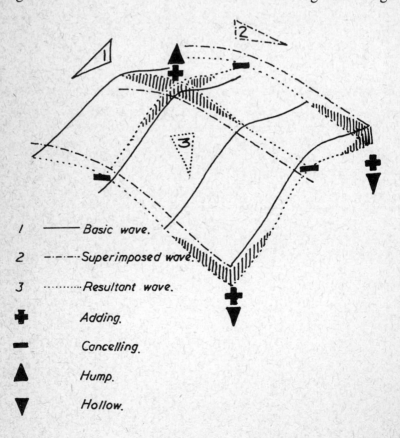

1 ——— Basic wave.

2 —·—·— Superimposed wave.

3 ············ Resultant wave.

✚   Adding.

━   Cancelling.

▲   Hump.

▼   Hollow.

phase momentarily. The troughs of each form add together to form a deeper trough, being in phase. However, where the crest of one wave crosses the trough of the other the wave forms cancel each other out being out of phase. The resulting sea is not one of lines of crests moving one way cutting lines of crests moving in another, but a hump and hollow sea with a regular diamond pattern linking each hump and surrounding each hollow.

Wave reflection

A simple wave form approaches a solid breakwater at an angle. A wave crest will meet the wall of the breakwater and be reflected from it in such a way that the angle of incidence of the wave crest is equal to the reflected angle of the wave crest. As the reflected wave retreats from the wall it meets the next wave crest and doubles

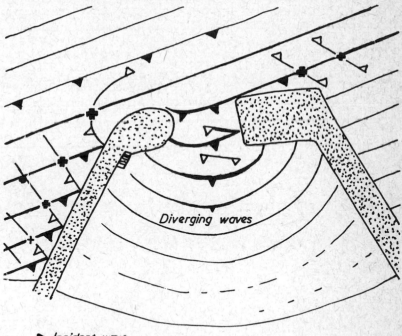

Diverging waves

▶ Incident wave.

▷ Reflected wave.

Wave reflection

with it. When the waves are big enough there is a powerful
collision throwing tons of water high into the air. This is called
'clapotis'. If the wave crest is parallel to the wall of the breakwater
the collision takes place half a wave length away from the wall.
If the wave crest is angled the collision takes place further away
from the wall but with less force. When the incident and reflected
waves meet at an angle, the resulting towering waterspout
advances shorewards, parallel to the breakwater wall. This is
quite fearful and canoeing would be impossible. However, on a
calm day by the beach when one is seeking some surfing fun and
the waves are too small, it is possible, if there is such a wall from
which waves may reflect, to find useful humps of water trundling
shorewards, parallel to the wall, which can provide enough
sport for most people.

A knowledge of the nature of reflected waves and the explosive
nature of colliding waves, with which are associated relatively calm
'nodal lanes', can assist one to seek favourable eddy currents close
to a cliff without being caught in the smash of the backlash.
Variations of a few yards closer to or further out from the re-
flecting surface may make a great difference to the handling of
the canoe.

Wave refraction, convergence

All wave forms obey certain natural laws and reflection and
refraction are common to many studies. Refraction takes two
forms—convergence and divergence. In convergence the wave is
concentrated at a point, and the wave height at the point of
convergence may be very great, breaking and dangerous, whilst
a few yards away the waves are quite small and easy to handle.

A simple wave form advances and passes over a submerged
hump or sandbank on the sea bottom so that the critical depth
for that wave is greater than the depth of water available. The
wave, as it enters the shallower water at the front of the hump,
will feel bottom, slow down and break. The line of the crest will
be bent, the concave face toward the natural focus of the waves
on that hump. The deep water wave will continue unabated, but
the shallow water wave will be bent and dissociated from the rest
of its crest. The leading or seaward edge of the hump will be safe
enough to paddle by but the tail end of the hump will have bowling

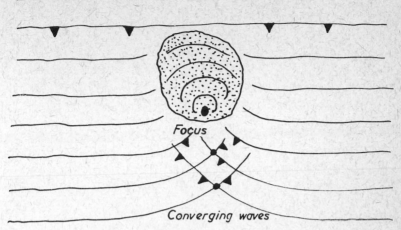

Focus

Converging waves

Wave refraction, convergence

waves coming to a focus there with much turbulence and clapotis. It is possible for a small wave to turn around completely and go back out to sea meeting the rest of itself on the way out. The sides of the hump may be fairly free from any wave form as the waves are being 'stretched' just there because of the focusing effect of the hump. Close to the tail of the hump waves which have come from the far side of the hump will be bent across to emerge on the opposite side of the tail causing a cross sea.

Generally, a canoeist should treat all such underwater obstructions with respect, having regard to boxing waves, state of the tide and so on; generally it is better to pass to the seaward side of such a source of turbulence.

Wave refraction, divergence

Waves may diverge if there is shallow water on each side of a deep water channel, as in a harbour entrance. The simple wave form comes in parallel to the shore and enters the deep channel. Inside the channel entrance the water deepens all round like the inside of a bottle. The wave crest on each side of the opening is either broken, slowed or reflected by the jaws of the opening. The crest runs uninhibitedly into the deep channel and curves around because its sides are subject to the shallow water drag at the sides. The length of the wave crest is extended in a typical arc form and the energy of the wave is now dispersed over a much greater length of wave crest. The energy per foot length of wave rapidly becomes much less.

A canoeist in the harbour will find little waves, very gentle in their effect. But paddling towards the entrance he will butt into the waves and find that each one is much more powerful than the preceding one. In the mouth he may find that what seemed possible two waves back is now quite impossible. Also in the mouth there will be the cross waves of the reflections and refractions at the mouth apart from the sudden exposure to the full energy of the sea.

Breaking waves

Breaking waves take two major forms—surf and dumpers. The dumper is destructive but the surf provides the fun. Of course, there is a wide range of wave forms between perfect examples of one and the other.

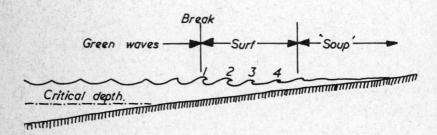

Surf

Surf is found on a gently sloping beach with a gradient of about one in twenty. The waves come toward the beach in straight lines and when they reach the critical depth they break in a gently curling wave. The wave begins to break at one place or another and the breaking peak progresses along from one end or another. The break usually begins where the water is slightly less deep than elsewhere. The unbroken waves are called green waves and most surfing takes place on the green waves if they are big enough. The break itself is a most violent experience. Later, as the dying wave struggles up the shore, the white foam of the break and of previous breaks merges into a general smother of white water called the 'soup'. It is not much use for real surfing but it is useful for novices to experience wave movements.

When looking at a beach one should watch for a good fifteen minutes so as to assess the surf overall. A three line break is good surf usually, but this may extend in a few minutes to ten line surf as a box arrives or when a half tide reef goes under. One should be watching for the effects of boxing on the surf. Beaches have all manner of surprises to offer.

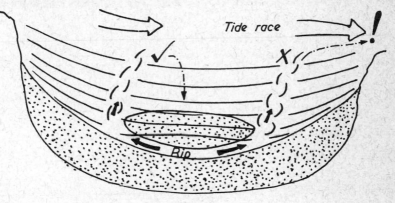

Rip channel.

Tide rip

The tide rip is usually associated with a surfing beach. Likely places for rips to begin may be spotted at low tide when the beach may be seen to have a low hump breaking the generally smooth rise. At the shoreward side of the hump is a shallow depression which is the channel and which curves away to one or both sides of the hump. When the tide rises it tends to cut off the hump by swilling around behind it. Later, as the surf comes foaming in, the water in the 'soup' area is actually being carried up the beach by the action of the waves and, of course, it must go back to sea. It runs back not directly outwards but sideways along the rip channel in the form of an alongshore current, quite strong enough to carry off swimmers and move canoes away from their surfing site to the danger of nearby swimmers. A rip is a useful thing to have, because outgoing canoeists seeking surf may take the express ride out behind the break in the flattened and less rough rip channel where it eventually swings out to sea. One must beware of tidal influence taking charge and carrying the canoeist out of the rip channel round the headland into a tide race and probable overfalls.

Dumpers

In this case, the waves run in unchecked and with their energy unspent until within a few yards of the beach. The bottom then rises abruptly, and the critical depth is reached in a moment. The break is towering and immediate all along the length of the wave.

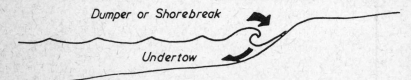

The almost explosive violence of a dumper dropping a canoe onto a beach will smash the canoe in an instant.

It is easy to spot a dumper beach by looking at it when the tide is out. If there is a distinct shelf at high tide mark, especially where a sand beach gives way to a steep shingle beach, then expect dumpers at high tide. Such steep beaches are called storm beaches and are the result of very high winter tides with onshore storm force winds piling in and churning up the whole beach, moving large stones and rocks and piling them up at the far reach of the tide. Some beaches may offer shelves at other stages of the tide, or rock outcrops which when covered may interrupt a line of crest and cause it to break and dump whilst the rest of the crest runs on unchecked to a good surfing beach.

If one is not wary about dumper beaches it is tempting to believe that the single line of breaking water is a preferable alternative to many lines of breaking waves. This is not so as the whole energy of the wave is released in such a short time that destructive forces result. When out at sea the dumper beach can be distinguished by the white smoke of spray blowing from the crests close in by the shore. The dumper may also be known as shorebreak.

Undertow

The undertow is the inevitable associate of the dumper wave. The water is dumped up on the beach and must return to the sea.

It is such a steep beach that it goes out directly toward the sea and seethes back under the next towering wave, sucking with it gravel and rocks and people. Whereas the rip is long and fairly gentle, the undertow is short and exceptionally powerful. It sucks back under the next wave then dissipates its power within a few yards. Its action is like that of a weir stopper of great power and rhythmic action. A swimmer in it is alternately swept onto the beach, dumped with great force onto gravel, then dragged back under the next crunching blow to be swept up and slammed down onto the beach over and over again.

If one must land on a dumper beach, release knee braces, spray deck, etc., just off the break then wait until the next wave is under the canoe so that the crest is only just in front of the cockpit. Sprint in, bows high, anticipate the drop and crash, leap out at once, grab the canoe and run. You have about three to six seconds to make your leap and run. If the bows drop, you are too far forward and a bone-jarring 'pearl dive' may happen, the feet may burst through the footrest and the canoeist be trapped in the wedge of the bows. Of course, a big dumper may be ideal for a pearl dive with loop and spin out onto the beach but it must be just right.

Judging wave height

Judging wave height is a skill which requires practice and experience. When sitting in a canoe it is easy to relate the wave height to one's own standing height and so a crest which is above eye level enough to cut out the view of the horizon, is called a six-foot wave when really it is only about thirty inches high.

Stand at the edge of the water and look out to sea at the horizon. Observe the height of the wave in the break. If the breaking wave just cuts out the horizon line of sight then the wave is about eye level above water level. Remember also that the crest rises and the trough falls from the mean level, so a wave crest judged to be 6 ft. when seen from the shore may in fact be about 8 ft. in the break. If the wave is lower than that, squat down so that the eye level is about half what it was. Again the wave height may be estimated.

Generally speaking, if the wave is about 4 to 6 ft. high it is suitable for experienced canoeists who can handle a roll and a loop both ways. If it is between 18 in. and 4 ft. high it is for improvers wishing to practise rolling in the rough, who may, incidentally, perform a loop on a big wave. Less than 18 in. waves are about right for novices providing they have a strong high draw stroke.

Out at sea, wave height is important in the context of communication with the group. If the horizon is in view (even if only just) at all times then visual contact is easy. However, the crest height need only rise by 2 or 3 in. and visibility is suddenly reduced from many miles to a wavelength. Partners in the adjacent troughs are completely out of sight and communication depends on chance sightings when on adjacent crests.

Chapter 12

Sea Techniques: Surfing

Surfing has greater affinity with river canoeing than with the deep water techniques required beyond the break. It is possible to go afloat safely on the surf with no knowledge of weather, tides, races and all the many complications which a deep water canoeist must consider. However, surf canoeing requires strong canoes and rapid reactions rather than careful thought; techniques are emerging so that, where once a surfing run was a step into the deep end, the canoeist can now go afloat and say with some certainty, 'There I will loop, there waltz and there roll six times'. Even so, there is about surfing a sense of the controlled accident which appeals to some and not to others.

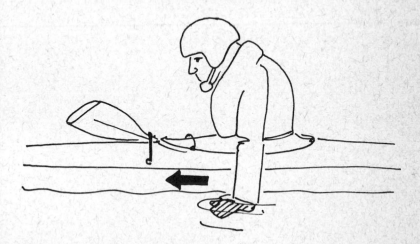

Going afloat

Going afloat

Putting on the canoe is a lengthy process particularly with those which have very tight spray decks, and so one must try to adjust the canoe undisturbed by water flow and then to go afloat whilst in the canoe. From a beach it is better to wait until a box is just dying away, put the canoe in about one inch of water, step in and sit down. The canoe grounds as one steps in so stability is no problem. Be sure that the hull of the canoe is not resting on some sharp or knobbly obstacle. The paddle may be rested alongside but beware the return flow of the receding wave washing it away. It is best to trap it under the foredeck elastic. Adjust spray deck and release strap and wait until the next box begins to arrive. As soon as a wave swills about the canoe, push down on the sand on either side with the knuckles and hutch the hull forward. This requires a good deal of arm and body strength, but most people can manage it. As the wave recedes again, rest and wait for the next. If you have chosen your moment correctly, two or three waves should see you afloat and in full control from the very beginning. The seal launch may be a life saver in some cases when a landing on and re-launching from a cliff face ledge is essential.

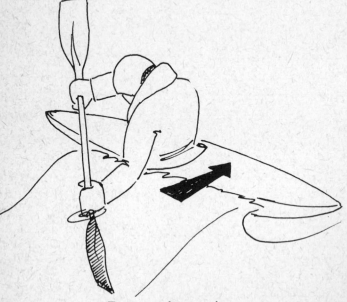

Draw stroke practice

Draw stroke practice

The novice should now go a short way into the 'soup' and lay the canoe parallel to the small, incoming waves. As the wave arrives alongside put the paddle blade over the back of it in a high draw position and lean slightly onto it as the wave passes under the hull. The tiny, but distinctive, wave currents will be felt pulling first one way and then the other. As the wave passes away to the shoreside, lift the paddle out and wait until the next one. When the timing of balance is mastered, go deeper into the bigger waves until one is lying right under the break of a 3 ft. wave. This is when it becomes exciting. It is not possible to reach over the crest of such a wave for the back of it so one stabs into the heart of the wave with the blade in the high draw position, using maximum power and lie-in to the wave face.

'Soup' riding

If the waves are high and wild, surfing experience may be gained in the little waves as they thrash into the beach well inside the break. Riding the green waves and through the break should be left until the waves generally are not larger than 2 ft. high. Occasionally, with a sea running diagonally to the beach, it is possible to find small gentle surf just inside the wave-side headland with surf gradually increasing in height as one moves away from the shelter of the headland.

Penetrating surf

If there is a rip to ride out beyond the break, then use it. If not, keep the canoe at right-angles to the oncoming waves which initially will be churning and frothy. It is a good plan to keep one's head down and forward, preferably with nose and mouth pressed against the top of the lifejacket, as the wave arrives seething along the foredeck to burst upwards in spray as it strikes the front edge of the cockpit rim. A face full of vigorous spray may be most hurtful to the nasal sinuses. As the wave strikes the bows, lean well forward in an attacking attitude and place the paddle well into the heart of the wave face. As the wave sweeps by bring the paddle blade back toward the lift-out position, keeping it deep so that the bows drop into the next trough as the wave goes by and the paddle lifts out ready for the steady paddling rhythm. It is

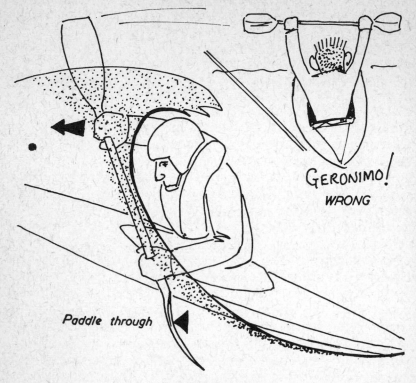

GERONIMO!
WRONG

Paddle through

Penetrating surf

faulty and an absolute give-away that you are a beginner without experience to lift up your paddle over your head in the position known amongst canoeists as a 'Geronimo'!

As the larger waves are met it may be a good idea to wait until a box subsides before entering the break line. Sometimes, if there is a change in the sea bottom level which develops a cross sea, it may be really easy to sneak out through the valleys that the interfering part of the cross sea presents. There may be really big surf close by, but an eye for interfering and doubling wave forms will show the way.

If one is faced with a towering, curling wave a reverse loop is quite probable; a quick look round before the monster strikes is no bad idea so that some idea of the whereabouts of other canoeists and swimmers may be gained. In order to reduce the chances of a reverse loop, speed into the wave is essential. An air of grim determination is helpful, a do or die purpose to go *through* it. Sprint into it with Shakespeare's Henry V speech, 'Once more unto the breach . . .' in mind, lunge at the heart of the green wall, dig into it shoulder deep and keep the weight as far forward as possible, head tucked in, the whole body braced onto the deep paddle as in a high draw taken forward. The experience is quite frightful, but exhilarating afterwards. The rocket-like leap out of the back of the wave may unseat you and the desire to stop paddling and rest may be strong, but resist it and sprint again because the next great green wall is humping up to pound you to pieces if you let go your grip and purpose. This, as in climbing, is the crux and only a super effort will take you through. A canoe out of control crashing in, broached to the break, is cutting a fourteen-feet wide track across the sea like a marine Boadicea's chariot. Swimmers and other canoeists have been injured by canoes out of control.

Having made the exit, go out well beyond the break for fear a box will take the break line back behind you. Sit and recover. Look about and weigh up the onset of the boxes, picking out the big ones coming; this should be possible as the bigger ones show as darker walls advancing in the general movement of the sea. One should have about 30 to 60 seconds warning of the arrival of the waves.

Picking a ride

Having decided that the big ones are arriving, check the sea in front and to each side for the presence of other surfers and swimmers ahead. Most canoeists will be jockeying about around the same distance out from the shore and to have surfers each side of one within less than 30 ft. is an indication to miss the wave that they take and ride the next in. If possible do this by agreement. Say, 'This is mine!' Or give way if the other fellow yells first. Also remember that the bigger waves tend to arrive two or three back after the first of the big waves. The less able should take the earlier wave or wait until the box has nearly passed.

As the wave preceding the selected wave surges under start to paddle steadily forward, but do estimate the position of the break. If to paddle forward would put you under the break then a snap action loop is almost inevitable. In that case it is better to remain still, and only to sprint as the stern rises to the wave face. The acceleration as the wave picks the canoe up is immediate and some canoes will broach immediately. Slalom canoes will broach or lie parallel to the wave very easily. Straight-running canoes should give the straight-in line 'big-gun' ride of the board riders.

The ride

On a green unbroken wave the ride will be fast—about 10 to 15 m.p.h.—and the hull will be planing. It is possible to stop by paddling backwards up the wave and back over the top or by dropping in and rolling. I would estimate that the subjective thrill of speed on a 6 ft. wave is about the same as that to be had on a fast motor car weaving its way along a twisting mountain road. Control may be had from stern rudder steering strokes, high draw strokes or hanging draw strokes.

In the break, as the saying goes, 'All Hell breaks loose!' The need to be locked into the racketing cockpit is very great. Spray hisses by and the rumble of the breaker is right around and underneath; one takes a hard rattling ride. The direction is variable and swings instantaneously and with vicious force. For example, a broached ride left with a high draw right to hold it tweaks into a stern first reverse slide right, again with the high draw right.

Stopping is now impossible for, do what you will, right way up or wrong way up, the crashing force of the energy of the wave has been released and will expend itself within the next minute or two. This is the point when accidents and collisions occur because one cannot act, but only re-act. As the great energy of the break eases away and leaves the 'soup' it may then be possible to direct matters again, and to regain steering and stopping power. The only way to avoid an accident just after the break may be to spot the obstacle a hundred yards ahead when riding the green wave and to pull out then, thus avoiding the break.

Controlling the direction, green wave

Out beyond the break is the safer place to be, with control reasonably easy. Various standard presentations occur and various perches on the wave are found.

1. On flat water with the canoe level, steering is normal.

2. In the trough of the wave with the canoe level, steering is difficult.
3. On the crest with the canoe level, steering is very easy.
4. On the back of the wave steering is wallowing and slow.
5. On the face of the wave steering is delicate, quick and requires a sensitive touch.
6. It is possible to be low on the wave, centre on the face or high in the crest. If the bows lift, the wave has gone by and to regain it is not possible.
7. Position on the wave may be adjusted by paddling forward if high and wishing to be lower or paddling backwards if low and wishing to be higher.

Therefore, assuming that one is centre on the face and wishes to control direction the various main possibilities follow:

1. Straight run in, right-angles to the wave—a 'big gun' ride.
2. Broached, sideways run, high draw dead centre.
3. If (1) is the case, steering is by light stern rudder, or body and hull lean. The canoe will turn away from the direction of lean and the back of the blade may be used very lightly on the side away from the turn to retain balance. If left too long this turns into a roll over the paddle.
4. Possible moves are:
   (a) Forward, left and right turns.
   (b) Reverse, left and right turns.
   (c) Turn followed through into broached ride.
5. If (2) is the case, steering is different. Balance is held by a high draw into the face of the wave. Apart from moving in sideway the canoe is moving along the face of the wave so this is faster over the water than a 'big gun' ride.
6. The steering in the high draw position is done by moving the point of application of the blade either forward or backward relative to the canoe.
7. Left side of canoe leading, right high draw.
   (a) Turn into stern first ride and perhaps back through the wave bow first, high bow rudder right.
   (b) Turn back to 'big gun' ride, hanging draw right rear.
8. Right side of canoe leading, left high draw.

(a) Turn into wave, left bow rudder, leaving stern first ride or break-back.

(b) Turn away from wave, left high draw, bow first ride.

9. Waltzing. This is done by beginning in the centre face of the wave, forward straight run.

(a) Right (say) bow rudder.

(b) Right high draw.

(c) Right high bow rudder (right high telemark).

(d) Stern first ride, switch balance to left, left reverse hanging draw.

(e) Left high draw.

(f) Left hanging draw, or stern rudder, bows first again.

(g) Rotation may be clockwise or anti-clockwise.

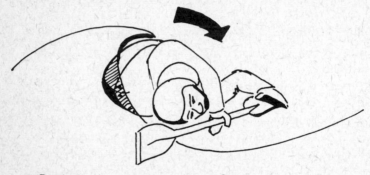

Rolling with wave : down right Steyr.

Rolling

Rolling in the rough—the natural instinctive roll—is only achieved by regular practice in natural conditions. Roll in pools on the river then roll in a rock-free spout of fast water. One soon learns to roll across a stream, down upstream and up downstream. Similarly, the easiest rolls are wave assisted. Sit in the 'soup' where the waves are about 2 ft. high, the bottom rock free and the water about 2 to 3 ft. deep. Line up the canoe parallel to the wave and start by high draw practice, pulling the canoe sideways through the wave. This is a good beginning point for novices in the surf in any event. When ready, wind up for the roll and have the paddle on the shore side. Roll over the paddle, down shore-side, up sea-side. It will be found that this is very easy requiring the minimum of power. Rolling the wrong way is not possible.

Alternatively go out towards the break, pointing directly at the towering breaker (but not right under it); just after it breaks capsize as it thunders over. Roll up in the quiet water behind. If one does it under the break one experiences a capsize, a vast plucking up sensation and a half reverse loop completed to emerge dazed and elated, right way up, riding the crest. First World War aviators called it the Immelman turn with an outside loop.

A week surfing, as at the British Canoe Union surfing week each year in Cornwall during September, when the big breakers roll and the 'bluebirds' soar in, will begin with much rolling practice before one is released to play with the surf. A free running canoe, because of a bail-out in the break, is dangerous and bad manners. Apart from which, one may be right in line with the next surf riding GRP projectile as one lies in the water.

Looping

Looping requires waves a little higher than half the length of the canoe. Much depends on the shape of the canoe, the shape of the wave and the exact point at which one picks up the wave. It is possible to ride a green wave in then edge forward and bows down into a forward loop, or go in for the instantaneous forward loop by awaiting the pick-up right under the break.

The better canoe to begin looping in is the 8 ft. baths canoe because it is easy to roll and is ultra-sensitive to the paddle. In looping, the bows dip down under the advancing face of the wave. The canoe goes vertical and one pitches forward over the bows into the passing crest of the wave. The baths canoe, being so short, soon loses its bows in little waves and the gentle flop over forwards is easy to experience and think about. A roll follows naturally and easily. The experience may be had in quite small, 3 ft. waves, with little energy and small risk.

A full size loop in a full size canoe begins with the forward slide down the wave face as the crest is beginning to break. As the bows slide under one should lean forward. A lean back will delay the loop or, perhaps, turn it into a 'skyrocket'. Having rolled over forward, the crest surges up about the canoe putting the bows 6 to 8 ft. under and subject to an overall, crushing pressure of a ton or more. The vertical acceleration is considerable and the canoe whips over into the upside down position, either being left behind in the trough ready for the roll or carried forward on a big one for the next half loop. Whether a half loop followed by a half roll should be called a loop or half loop is not certain. A full 360 deg. loop may be called a whole loop or a double loop. Call it what you like, it really is a most unusual and exhilarating experience.

Looping may be done forward or backward, from the ride or on the pick up, double or single, preceded by a capsize or finished by the roll. Do try it sometime, but wear lifejacket and helmet and have able watchers ready to pull you out if in real difficulty. All manner of awkward situations are possible:

PEARL DIVE. In this, the bows go under in shallow water and stop as they dig into the sand or bang against the rock. The deck may burst under the strain, the bows shatter, or footrest collapse. In any event it is a nasty experience. One is left cocked up on end and there is only one way out—down. The energy which must be absorbed by the footrest as one 14 stone body travelling at 15 m.p.h. comes suddenly to a halt whilst braced on it is very great.

DIVE AND SPIN-OUT. This begins as a pearl dive but the water is deep enough to reduce much of the force of the impact. The canoe wheels up and over into a loop but the stern does not go right over the bows but slides away to one side tracing out the surface of a cone with the bows as the apex. If one is quick and balances exactly right, the canoe is spun around in the upright position through 180 deg. as the loop through 180 deg. is taking place. One lands right way up, surfing in backwards, bows having risen from the bottom as the loop was completed.

SKYROCKET. The approach is normal, the loop begins but the bows just clip the bottom, stopping dead almost in the upright position. The wave passes by and under, and the canoe, subjected to the vast squeezing pressure from deep under the crest, lurches out of the back of the wave and soars into the sky leaving the water completely or with just about a foot of the bows left in the water. Anticipating a dive and spin out, one may have begun the spin, to find to one's horror, that one isn't going over but is crashing down from 6 or 8 ft. above the water, upside down.

TRAMPOLINE. A man whose ability with a canoe in surf is quite extraordinary and is matched by his agility on the trampoline, reckons that many of the trampoline moves may be translated into canoe surfing moves. That is not my line of work at all but it opens up some interesting avenues for exploration.

Chapter 13

Sea Techniques: Deep Water

Deep water canoeing is likely to satisfy a different person from one who enjoys surfing. Deep water canoeing is emphatically an exercise which demands knowledge, thought, and planning. Careful preparation is necessary if one is to be prepared for the unexpected things that turn up at sea. Having gone afloat, however, certain techniques are possible, and should be used.

Going afloat

As with an aircraft, the danger time is at take off and landing. Riding the frontier between air and water is hazardous enough, but to find hard resistant rock also in the conflict area is to find trouble. Surfing means launching from a beach, usually sand, and has already been described. Going afloat in deep water may mean a harbour launch, launching from a crevice in the rocks to battle out onto rough water against a cliff or emerging from an estuary into the sea over the bar where the river drops its load of silt and the waves feel bottom. Groups can launch one at a time down sloping concrete groins protecting promenades, at a 20 deg. angle to the horizontal, like children on the chute at the baths. Only GRP canoes, however, can stand up to that form of rough treatment. Enterprising canoeing requires original thought, strong canoes and able paddlers. Leave real sea canoeing to the skilled canoeist.

Steering a course

When at sea steady tidal movements will swing the canoe about and the movement will be almost imperceptible. It is possible to see the effects of such movements within moments of their beginning. Assuming that one has selected a course which will avoid headland races, bay rips in which the tide swings into one end of the bay and out of the other, and so on, from a chart or from inspection, then it should be possible to say to the members of the group, 'We will line up on the isolated rock off that headland and the white house on the headland beyond.' This is called taking a transit. By relying on parallax one may steer a dead straight course over the sea bottom and underlying currents will at once advertise their presence by the necessity to angle the canoe, as in a ferry glide, in order to remain on course. However, if one knows the bay very well it is possible at certain states of the tide to take, say, a half knot tidal sweep through the bay which in the course of an hour will add 1,000 yards to one's distance covered compared with the distance covered by a canoe which avoids the sweep by travelling in a straight line. Only local knowledge can help here.

On one occasion, I remember, it was possible to sense the beginning of a serious breakdown in plans by using transits. Between Ramsey Island and the Middle Bishop rocks there is a 5 to 7 knot race running for 7 or 8 miles and 2 miles wide. A transit was selected—the north cliffs of Ramsey and the white dot of a building on the mainland beyond. The canoes were angled about 45 deg. to the line of travel. A cross transit was taken on a skerry of rocks south of the line of travel and the South Bishop light further south still. Provided that the lighthouse closed the skerry from west towards the east and then opened out away from the skerry still towards the east, then we knew that we would still be moving eastwards.

The angle of the bows remained fairly constant toward Whitesand Bay but checks every few minutes on the cross transit showed that whilst the light was closing with the skerry and then lay behind it, a few minutes later it had opened out again *towards the west*. Our line of travel was still correct, our angle of canoe was right, but we were on our way back toward Middle Bishop! It can only be assumed that the increasing rate of run of the race as it picked up speed on the ebb to half tide had caused the whole pattern of the water movements to alter and to swing more westerly than had been the case 15 minutes earlier. That turned into an epic which ended in hitching a lift from a pleasure boat.

Navigation by transits is very simple and depends on clear vision. When I have been on the sea the mist has never yet cut me off from

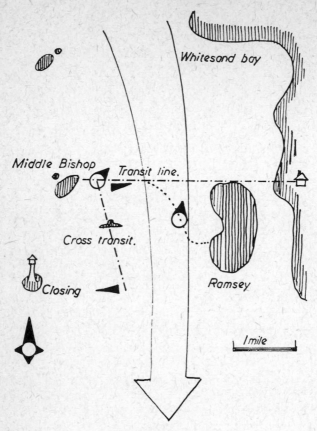

Steering a course

sight of land; however, I rarely go out more than a mile. There
have been times when, like the Scottish legend of the island which
rises out of the mists every hundred years to live for a day, I have
seen Inner Farne in full summer sunlight, its landward cliffs white,
the lighthouse brilliant white, the horizon sharply clear; a few
minutes later and the sea mists lie between the mainland and the
island and only the tip of the lighthouse appears. The mist literally
condensed in the air itself; there could not have been a movement
of air on such a still day to bring mist from far away. Others who
have been caught in these mists say that they are very confusing
and the only possible way to steer is by compass course or by

Ludwig Quist, Greenland seal hunter from the village of Igdlorssuit on Ubekendt Ejland. Note the kayak, a floating work bench. It has, starting from the bows, a bone toggle to finish off the covering of seal skin (taking four seal skins each worth about £5), a thong of hide for locating some item of equipment, the gun bag in which a 12 bore or 410, or even, for expert shots, a high velocity .22 is kept.

The high circular pan holds the coiled line to which the harpoon head is attached at one end, and the seal skin bladder (behind the cockpit) at the other. A killing club is to be seen slipped under the thongs on the foredeck, left of the cockpit.

Ludwig wears the sealskin trousers, mark of the hunter and straw packed seal skin boots laced and tied on. His paddle is unfeathered, made from a piece of wood 80 inches by three inches by one inch. It is tipped and edged with bone.

Ludwig was attached to the '66 geological expedition from St. Andrew's University, led by Senior Lecturer in Geology, Dr. Drever. The British Canoe Union was asked to find a suitable canoeist to accompany the expedition, and Chris Hare who took this photograph was selected.

observing the set of the sea waves and keeping the relation of canoe and crest line constant. To sit baking in a canoe on a still sea, the sun powerful through a thin surface mist and the sky blue overhead and yet to have no lateral vision because of grey mist, is a very isolating experience. Sound becomes distorted, and direction of sound variable.

Seal hunters in Greenland are reputed to be able to paddle their kayaks in a thick mist over miles of open fiord seas, and to tell, within a few hundred yards, where they are by the water pattern. Cliffs ashore will send out the faint tell-tale of reflected waves for a mile or two, and the experienced eye will see the influence. Another point of interest about the Eskimos is that they have journey sticks—faceted carved sticks which when looked at along their length faithfully reproduce the appearance of each headland and spur as it appears. One selects the edge of the stick appropriate to the coast being passed, squints along the journey stick and identifies each passing bay and headland. Nearby villages are spotted on the shank of the stick. That method depends on visual power too and gives rise to a truly practical folk art. I wonder if one could make journey sticks for North Wales? They float, too, if you drop them, never become soggy like a chart, and seem to me to be very practical, but only if one makes one's own.

Turning

The actual handling of the canoe on the sea is fairly easily managed; one does have a great deal of water room in which to move but it is surprising how some canoeists manage repeatedly to barge into someone nearby. It is probably the effect of the interfering wake forms. First, turn in the crest of the wave so that the immersed length of the canoe is at a minimum and one can see the transit marks most clearly in order to correct course. Turn in the crest, but in the trough let the canoe go as it pleases, within reason, as strong efforts to correct with the ends of the hull deeper in water than the centre will result in little turn and early exhaustion.

A rudder is very useful in the sea for turning, especially with the longer, kayak, type of hull which is better for efficient travel over long distances. Slalom canoes may be improved in the sea by strapping skegs under the rear of the hull or even by devising end caps complete with pintles and stock for hanging a rudder.

In a cross wind on open water the slalom type of canoe will swing and twirl about the sea in a most frustrating way. Usually the waves will be running with crests at right-angles to the wind and to paddle across this requires constant powerful draw strokes to pull the bows through each advancing wave; the bows, tending to dig deeper than the stern, allow the stern to drift away downwind, or catch the crest current and pay-off downwave. One never knows whether the little fiend is going to run surfing downwind or wallow, weathercock fashion, upwind. One usually ends up using great sweep strokes on the upwind side which become very tiring. An offset paddle grip, long lever to windward is a useful aid. Alternatively, when the sea is very tumbled and confused, the slalom canoe properly handled is very responsive and stable and great fun if covering distance is not important. Short choppy waves are quite normal on open lakes as well as the open sea.

Balance

Balancing the canoe in waves is a simple matter once one learns to lean toward the nearest wave and keep a steady paddling rhythm and an eye on the horizon. Most of the turning influences on a canoe hull may be anticipated at sea as on a river. Balance, which is associated with every turning movement, is easier as soon as one has learned to roll; one therefore worries less, tension is eased and the full power of the muscles may be released in the paddling effort with improved reaction time to disturbance of balance.

Currents

A knowledge of currents is helpful before one begins to go on the sea. On a river the current flow is easily seen and the effect is one of rapid turning in the horizontal and vertical planes. The effects of currents at sea, though great, are so subtle that they cannot be seen, only sensed. The result is an easy or a difficult trip depending on whether the current was a help or a hindrance. Sea currents affect duration, river currents affect balance.

All water obeys natural laws. If it swills past an obstruction an eddy current will form behind the obstacle. This eddy will be in a horizontal and a vertical plane. Covered obstacles set up predominantly vertical eddies; exposed obstacles set up horizontal eddies. The obstacle need not be isolated, it can be part of a continuing land, a river bank or a mainland. Jutting crags, skerries of rock, reefs or inward curving bays away from the line of the current will induce eddy currents to run against the general direction of the current.

When at sea, especially when traversing a headland, look out for the way the tidal currents move. It is possible to be paddling with a cross transit on some marks inland and to find that the marks open out very, very slowly despite a steady paddling effort. One way to check is to stop paddling until all way is off the boat and one is moving with the water. Observe the landmarks—the cross transit marks—and see which way they are drifting. The apparent direction of movement of the rearward or furthest mark indicates the direction of drift of the canoe.

If the drift is unhelpful, weigh up the surroundings. If there is an island a short way seawards tuck in behind it just as one would on a river, but look out for whirling eddies. Skokholm Island in South Wales has a 'Mad Bay' just off Wildgoose Race. One can guess why it received that name—Reed's Nautical Almanak singles out Wildgoose Race as being the most dangerous in the whole of the Bristol Channel. I hope to go there one day to look at it and wonder.

If there is no island go towards the mainland. However, an estimate of the nature of the race is important. If one is coming into a bay then the race may be a round-the-bay tidal drift, developing into a rip or race just off the headland. In that case it would be advisable to go well out into the bay away from the maximum rate of flow of the tide. If the race is off a cliff headland then an attempt to 'tuck in' to the eddies flowing right under the cliff face may be the better course of action. However, just under the face is where the reflected waves bang about and clapotis occurs. Reefs are crossed, landing is probably impossible and flares for help might not be seen from a lookout immediately above because of the bulge of the cliff.

The questions which present themselves at sea are really quite involved and decisions must be made which take into account the resources of the party. This is why it is necessary to stress that sea canoeing is for experienced canoeists, or at least, able canoeists with proper equipment and a full working knowledge of rescue techniques and under the direction of an experienced leader.

The subjective feeling of satisfaction is, I find, very strong after nearly every sea canoeing trip I make. One supposes that decision-making is as necessary for the mind as exercise is for the body.

Wind blasts and williwaws

Slocum, in his record of a single handed journey around the world, described the shattering effects of downblasts of wind from the mountains of Tierra Del Fuego. There is also such a place just off the north west cliff of the Great Orme. When a north westerly gale, upwards of force eight on the Beaufort Scale, is blowing, freak gusts of wind, whirling devils which shriek above the general howl of the wind on the water, rip twisting down from the crags and their effect is like the downblast of a helicopter rotor on the water. These williwaws flatten the canoeist and 'big digs' support strokes are very necessary. Strong, up to force six, winds are found over the open sea and may be tackled by experienced canoeists; but one should be aware that where land and air meet big eddies are set in motion and when these meet the sea, wind speeds far in excess of force six (up to 30 m.p.h.) winds may be briefly experienced. Other places around the British Isles will present their peculiar difficulties and local knowledge is the only way to spot them, apart from a general 'nose' for wind and weather.

Exhaustion

One should never come off the sea feeling anything more than a pleasant muscular tiredness and a feeling that it would have been possible to do it all over again straight away. If your group crawls up the beach 'shattered' then check your planning. The sea is very demanding and the penalties for simple errors of judgment or lack of care may be very serious.

Never be tied to a timetable—to hurry at sea is to ask for trouble. It may be necessary to run for cover and land in a totally unexpected place so that the land-based party misses you altogether. The tides turn every 6¼ hours and the impossible headcurrent may turn into a free ride home a few hours later.

Nevertheless, you will become exhausted because it is only when one is tried beyond the previously known limits of endurance that one learns what can be done. 'Be prepared' is the best advice.

Chapter 14

Deep Water Rescue

This section deals with an aspect of the sport which has developed in the last two years and which now is essential reading for the instructor who takes a group out onto deep open waters. The range and potential of sea canoeists has been vastly increased by new methods. The Eskimo roll is always the first line of defence in disastrous moments and if these new methods, including the roll, are not practised regularly in difficult conditions, then my advice is, don't take up sea canoeing.

Oliver Cock, the National Coach for the BCU, was the first to spread these ideas widely and as a result many canoeists tried new ideas. Some of these bordered on lunacy, others were better in certain circumstances than the old methods. The ideas were tried out at Atlantic College in South Wales, on the Solent and the Hamble where there are sea canoeing schools and in many other parts of the country including the North East where the winds blow cold and the sea runs lumpy.

The accent is definitely on skill in rough waters, which is where most accidents happen. The smooth waters which groups of beginners usually seek present little difficulty. However, there is one rescue method—swimmer to canoeist—which can be used for rolling instruction and which may save a life some day in a swimming bath. Many teachers are using school baths for canoeing instruction these days.

FAIL SAFE

This aspect of canoeing rescue is an attitude of mind like never chiselling towards one's person when woodworking. When setting up a rescue sequence make sure that, if you tackle it alone, you *know* you can do it and that no sudden freak wind is likely to whip

162

up and cause trouble, or that you and the person you are trying to save will drift into trouble. A rescuer is very likely to put down his paddle and it is a good idea to slip it under an elastic stretched across the foredeck just in front of the cockpit. In the event of a sudden capsize during the effort of lifting, which may be quite heavy, the paddle may be lost and the rescuer be unable to roll and bingo!—two people to be rescued.

If two canoes are laid parallel alongside, the first rescuer makes the effort to lift the capsized canoe whilst the second rescuer lies across the deck of the first and steadies both his own and the other canoe. A raft of two canoes is very stable. I have never seen one overturned yet—provided that they are held together. Therefore, if one has a patient in the water to be rescued, and two rescuers, it is clear that one should never go onto deep and open waters without there being three in the party.

LESS THAN THREE THERE SHOULD NEVER BE.

Coming within the scope of fail safe is the necessity for a strong canoe which will stand up to the heavy strains of either being lifted across another canoe whilst waterlogged or of supporting another canoe which is heavy with water. The most recent slalom-type canoes, which are often used on the sea on short trips, are built down to a competitive weight with a consequent reduction of deck strength. A lightweight canoe may not support the weight of a heavy rescue. Such a canoe should, if in GRP, be made with deck stiffening ribs or extra laminations of glass. 2 oz. lay-up will do for most purposes, but 3 or even 4 oz. lamination is indicated for rescue potential. If your canoe is to perform on the sea ask the manufacturers to stiffen the foredeck, at least. Usually they will and they rarely charge extra. Extra deck stiffness will be obtained by extending the length of the block of polystyrene foam, which is often found in competition type canoes, braced between keel and deck ridge both fore and aft. This has a drawback in that it limits the amount of equipment that one may load into the canoe when camping, for example.

Two-canoe raft

This is used as a fail safe technique or to assist the person in the water to re-enter the canoe after it has been emptied. It should be practised often.

Two-canoe raft

1. If fail safe, both canoes are laid alongside, both pointing the same way.
2. If re-entry, the canoes are laid alongside, pointing opposite ways.
3. The second man reaches across the first canoe, and *lays his chest* on the deck of the canoe, the offside arm lying along the gunwale line.
4. The second man's canoe will now be laid over so that the water will be lapping the cockpit rim. A spray deck is essential.
5. The nearside hand grasps the cockpit rim of the canoe being supported.
6. Stability and firmness of the raft will not be achieved unless the chest presses heavily upon the first canoe. Any clearance between chest and deck allows the canoe being supported to wobble and this is disconcerting for the person performing the rescue, or re-entering the canoe.

Swimmer to canoeist rescue

This method developed generally after the Loughborough B.C.U. Coaching Conference of 1966. Problems were suggested and dealt with in various ways. This is one of the ideas so tried out: The canoeist is trapped in the canoe, inverted and unable to assist in any way. The rescuer is in deep water, has no means of assisting his lift and must have the patient above water in less than two minutes. Once you have righted the canoeist, mouth to mouth resuscitation may begin at once.

1. Swim quickly to the upturned canoe. Unlike the approach to the struggling swimmer there is no need to hold off for caution. Use the speed of the body and its momentum to carry it up over the bottom of the upturned canoe.
2. Reach down into the water and grasp the arm of the patient.

Swimmer to canoeist rescue

3. Ensure a firm grasp. There is no time for fiddling about. Pull the arm over the bottom of the canoe so that it rises from the water as the patient's body is pulled close to the deck of the canoe. This is very important as it reduces the effort required to right the canoe and patient.
4. Pull firmly and steadily at the arm. A heavy jerk could dislocate the shoulder of the patient.
5. The patient and his canoe will come upright and as they pass the flip-over point they come over with a rush.
6. To prevent the patient capsizing upon the rescuer, push upwards hard, thus sending yourself down into the water. Retain hold of the patient. This requires accurate timing and, of course, practice.

ESKIMO RESCUE

This technique is very useful in a group which is closely knit. The patient capsizes, thumps the bottom of the canoe to attract attention and waves his arms about, and someone nips up smartly to offer some part of canoe or paddle shaft on which to pull. It is essential that this should all take place within 6 or 7 seconds as few people will stay down longer than this unless they have confidence in the rescue being completed quickly. One may 'swim up' to obtain a breath of air. This confidence is only gained through practice. A firm spray deck is essential, of course.

Bow presentation

1. The patient capsizes, reaches under his canoe and thumps the bottom of the canoe with his hands. This makes a loud noise. He then waves his hands in the air *one each side*. There is a temptation to take one hand and place it ready on the spray deck release strap. It is in the nature of things that this will be the hand which is required to grasp the paddle shaft or bows of the rescuing canoe.

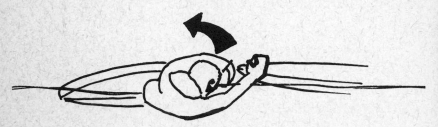

2. The rescuer must be able to manoeuvre his canoe accurately and quickly and a slalom type canoe is an advantage here. He swings his bows into the waving hand of the patient.
3. The rescuer must come close with care. The patient may decide to pop up for a breather before going down again to wait a little longer and to have a swiftly moving sharp end of the canoe rammed into one's nostril is a distressing experience (it has happened). Too quick an approach and injury may result; too slow and the patient bales out. Practice will help one to know how slow is too slow and how fast is too fast.
4. The patient will grasp the bows of the canoe and pull up. The weight must be transferred quickly and accurately from one hand to the other during the lift. If he lies forward and curled up the rotation is made easy. If he lies well back the rotation is easier, but only if the back of the head is touching the rear deck. In both cases co-ordination of the hands is a difficulty which can easily be sorted out by practising.

Paddle presentation

1. The first stages are as in bow presentation.
2. The rescuer comes alongside allowing a space of about 12 in. between the hulls of the two canoes.

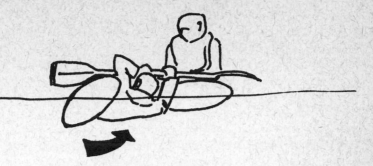

Paddle presentation

3. The rescuer puts his paddle across his own foredeck and the upturned hull of the other canoe. When the paddle is firmly placed he grasps the waving hand of the patient and guides it onto the paddle shaft. The patient then pulls on the shaft and pops up between the two canoes.

Assisted alongside lift

1. Rescuer comes alongside and either takes hold of the waving hand on the far side of the upturned canoe or reaches down into the water over the upturned hull of the canoe and takes hold of the patient's arm.
2. Rescuer hauls up and towards himself. This is a difficult lift as the two canoes are pulled hard towards each other, and the resulting friction between the hulls makes it difficult to rotate the upturned canoe. The patient can help by laying his head well back along the rear deck.

Assisted alongside lift

X method

On flat water when the patient has capsized neatly and left his canoe with no fuss and the upturned canoe is riding high on the water with little water trapped within it, the X method is indicated. It requires strength, speed and confidence and these are only achieved with practice.

X method

1. Arrange the rescuing canoe so that the bows of the upturned canoe are beside the cockpit, and the hull is at right angles to the upturned canoe.
2. Grasp the bows and lift them onto the foredeck of the rescuing canoe.
3. Pull hard immediately on the deck lines so that the upturned canoe slides quickly over the foredeck until the cockpit is laid across the foredeck of the rescuing canoe. If the cockpit of the upturned canoe is allowed to dwell half in and half out of the water, water will flow in and make rescue by this method impossible.
4. There is a moment when the cockpit rim of the upturned canoe reaches the edge of the rescuing canoe, and forms an obstruction to further progress. A sharp jerk with both hands on the cockpit rim of the upturned canoe will swing it further up onto the deck.
5. Continue the sliding up of the upturned canoe over the rescuing foredeck until a point of balance is reached. Sway the body weight in the direction that the upturned canoe is moving, the whole assembly will swing over like a see-saw and the contained water will be lifted up and swill out of the upturned cockpit. Tilt the other way once to make sure.
6. Note: If the rescuing canoe does not have a spray deck, the

water from the rescued canoe will flop into the rescuing canoe and cause difficulty.

7. Turn the emptied canoe over and slide it into the water alongside the rescuing canoe. The canoes should be pointing in opposite directions. A two canoe raft is now formed as previously described.

8. The patient re-enters his canoe by reaching across onto the cockpit of his own canoe from the side away from the rescuer. He kicks his feet until he lies along the surface of the water and then surges up onto his own canoe pulling himself over his cockpit. He may reach further across onto his rescuer's canoe to gain extra pull. Once across the cockpit he twists around or may even stand up with his hands on the rescuer's head as he makes himself comfortable in his own canoe.

TX method

It often happens, especially in rough water, that the upturned canoe becomes fairly well swamped and weighty with trapped water. An initial move to reduce the quantity of trapped water is required before using the X method. Methods of construction or the simple expedient of stuffing the whole canoe, except the part that one sits in, with buoyancy material will reduce the likelihood of this being necessary.

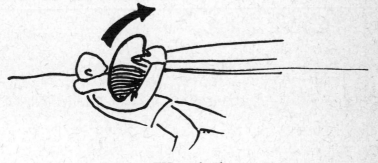

TX method

1. Rescuer turns the bows of rescue canoe towards the cockpit of upturned canoe.
2. Patient rotates upturned canoe until cockpit is tilted upwards and towards the rescue canoe.

3. The rescuing canoe is paddled forward so that the bows enter the cockpit hole. Gentle forward paddling strokes keep it there.
4. The upturned canoe is turned over onto the other canoe's bows. The patient reaches under his canoe and grasps the bows of the rescue canoe. The upper edge of his cockpit rim must not slip off the other canoe's bows.

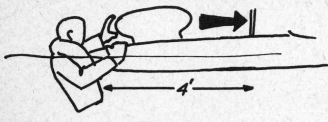

TX method

5. The patient lifts his canoe steadily upwards onto the bows of the rescue canoe. There will come a moment when he can, as water continues to spill out of his cockpit, place the lower edge of the cockpit up on to bows of the rescue canoe.
6. His canoe can now be pushed further onto the other's bows. Don't take it right up to the cockpit of the rescue canoe (as in the full X position) if it contains a great deal of water.
7. It should now be about 2 to 4 ft. onto the foredeck of the rescue canoe.
8. The patient goes to upper end of the uptilted canoe and pulls down. This is when the maximum crushing load is applied to the foredeck of the rescue canoe. A crunched canoe is not much use in a long paddle back to base. It has been calculated that upwards of two hundredweight is applied to the foredeck during the start of the see-saw action. The water rocks out.
9. The tipping out is completed much as in the X method.
10. Re-entry is done as previously described.

Note: Fail safe may be greatly increased by using two canoes rafted together to provide the lift. The load on the bows causes them to dip down, thus making the foredeck of the rescuing canoes into an inclined plane up which it is fairly easy to slide the upturned canoe. Big canoes with buoyant bow sections and canvas canoes

with light section deck beams are not suitable for this method as
the deck beams will smash under the load. Waves are often a help
during the tipping out action when it is found that the rescuing
canoe broaches to and the lower end of the rescued canoe is tilted
up by the face of the next wave, thus spilling its contents with little
extra load on the foredeck. Rescues in the fringe of the surf are
not possible, as the forward surge of the wave crests causes the
canoes to over-ride each other, in which case swim out to deep
water or pull in to the shore.

HI method

This is my own name for it. It was originally described by canoeists
from Ipswich (hence the *I*) and was demonstrated at the Coaching
Conference at Loughborough in April 1967. It has since been made
clear that the sea school at Hamble was using the method before
then, so the credit should be shared.

1. Some canoes may be supplied with buoyancy at one end only.
   GRP material being non-buoyant will sink and so the end
   without buoyancy will drift downwards as the other end rises up.
   Getting the *TX* to work on this is very, very difficult. The canoe

HI method

is obviously slightly more than half full of water (about 5 cwt).

2. Two rescuers line up, parallel, one each side of the capsized canoe.

3. The patient goes to the bows of one of the rescuing canoes and grasps the rim of the cockpit of his own canoe, now under water.

4. The two rescuers place their paddles across their foredecks, so that they and the paddles are at right-angles.

5. The bows of the upturned canoe are taken by one of the rescuers and pulled towards the paddle 'bridge', at the same time keeping the bows low in the water. The patient meanwhile lifts at the cockpit rim obtaining the upward pressure required by downward thrust on the bows of one of the rescuing canoes.

6. When the cockpit rim breaks water, air can flow in and water out. The patient braces his shoulder under the cockpit rim and so exerts a steady upward pressure causing the water to continue to spill out of the cockpit.

7. The rescuers meanwhile keep pulling the bows of the upturned canoe toward the paddle bridge. When the canoe is about level on the water, the deck is lifted onto the bridge and a steady pull, aided by a push from the patient, brings the upturned canoe into a see-saw position across the paddle bridge.

8. This method now differs in principle from the *TX* method, in that the patient causes the water to empty out by a rocking motion over the paddle shafts by thrusting his end upwards, obtaining the necessary lift from the bows of the rescuing canoe. The rocking out is done once or twice and the empty canoe turned right way up and placed back in the water. Re-entry is as before, or he may use the paddle bridge and climb in between the rescuing canoe and his own canoe by bracing the feet up on the paddle bridge and levering his backside over into the cockpit.

OTHER METHODS COMPARED

The first generally used method was the *H* method. This does not fail safe unless each of the two lifting rescuers is braced by a second man. This requires five people to be involved in the rescue. I do not like it now having failed on one rather important occasion to use it successfully. Others may not find it so objectionable. In this method two rescuers are parallel and at either end of the upturned canoe. They then make a dead lift of the heavy canoe which puts them off balance unless very careful.

The next methods to be used generally were the X and TX methods which took their names from the plan view of the operation. They both use a system of levers to reduce the effort required by a dead lift but both put crushing loads upon the deck of the rescuing canoe.

The latest method, the HI, uses a sophisticated system of levers, and the rocking out is done by lifting not by pulling down. Hence the load on the rescuing canoes is reduced.

When the patient re-enters the canoe he can do so either between the canoes—by pressing down on the canoes on each side of him— or by climbing across his canoe towards the rescuing canoe. The drawback of a between-canoe entry is that the swing and sway of two buoyant canoes on a choppy sea causes them to clash together with come force, and to have one's head between is to run the risk of getting a thick ear. Further, as one presses down whilst rising from the depths the canoes swing apart, unless the shoulder muscles are under powerful control, and one slides helplessly down again.

A paddle bridge giving support to the heels is useful for a between-canoe entry but the better method is to clamber onto the canoe from the outside—the effort of re-entry pulling the canoes together, not forcing them apart. One's ears retain their shell-like beauty also, but the lifejacket gets in the way.

It is clear that most canvas or folding canoes would lack the physical strength to stand up to the heavy strains involved in these methods so the techniques could not really develop until after the 'sixties began and GRP canoes were in plentiful supply.

WHICH METHOD?

The first thing to remember is that one has no choice of method unless each method has been practised. This requires repeated practice sessions in swimming baths, then on calm open waters, then on rougher open waters but never far from an easy swim to shore. The really important rescues which occur by accident must be left to the natural course of events. Be prepared.

Some methods throw all the effort on to the rescuer, others all on to the patient. Usually the patient is weakened already, hence the capsize, and the stunning cold of the water may further sap his strength to such an extent that helpful efforts are almost impossible. The swimmer-canoeist rescue puts all the load onto the rescuer as does the parallel Eskimo rescue.

The bow and paddle presentation Eskimo rescues put all the load on to the patient, but they are of necessity, quick.

The *X* method puts most of the load on to the rescuer; the patient is required only to scramble back into the canoe and that is not necessarily easy for unfit people or those with a low power-weight ratio in the arms.

The *TX* and *HI* methods require some co-operation from the patient.

It is worth remembering that a helpless patient may be assisted back into his canoe if a fit member of the party takes his place in the water as in the *HI* method. He can do the work necessary to empty the canoe, then by a system of levers and paddle bridges heave the patient back into the canoe and himself return to his own canoe for a deep water re-entry.

Chapter 15

Canoe Building in Glass Reinforced Plastics

There have been great developments in the practice of canoe building since this book was first published. Now it is proposed to apply standards to the construction of commercial canoes. The trade is applying its own standards through the British Canoe Manufacturers Association, which can be contacted through Frank Goodman, Valley Canoe Products, Private Road 4, Colwick Estate, Nottingham. The British Standards Committee is considering more general rules. Up-to-date information on these can be obtained from the British Canoe Union, 70 Brompton Road, London SW3 1DT.

There has been a great increase in the number of people who have moulds suitable for turning out GRP canoes. Twenty years ago, canvas covered canoes were to be found everywhere, as they are today. Ten years ago, the plywood canoe was developed and is found everywhere today. The GRP canoe is now taking its turn. What will be the favoured boat in another ten years time? Improvements on GRP are already being developed and used for canoe construction.

So much detail is necessary to cover the building of canoes in GRP that it would make a book in itself. Therefore this section will be a general outline of what may be done by the canoe building group.

WORKSHOP

The requirements given here have been found to be very useful but variations are quite possible. The important thing to remember is that the skilled GRP operator must use the room as a tool; he must be able' to raise and lower its temperature at will from 60 deg. F. to 80 deg. F. and alter the ventilation as required. Ideally, one should have three workshops: the polishing room, the laminating room and the finishing room, each one becoming progressively less dust free.

175

Requirements

1. Working area should be at least 20 ft. square and 15 ft. high.
2. Sink, hot and cold running water, nail scrubbing brushes, paper towels.
3. 13 amp power point.
4. Roof beams from which to sling moulds when making joints in mould/jig.
5. Opening windows.
6. Adjustable heat source.
7. Thermometer.
8. Floor covered with old cardboard packing cases, or plastic.
9. Long benches, 12 ft. by 2 ft. 6 in., two at least.
10. Smooth topped cutting bench for glass.
11. Low bench for mixing resins.
12. Small bench, 2 ft. 6 in. square, for holding cockpit mould.
13. Fire extinguishers beside door.

TOOLS

Power tools are recommended. These are not essential but they do make the greatest difference between a good job quickly done and a less good job slowly done.

1. Electric drill, $\frac{5}{16}$ in chuck, 2 speed.
2. Sanding disc, 5 in., discs 50 or 60 grit.
3. Orbital sander, pads 100 grit, 160 grit.
4. Spring balance to measure 10 lb. by 1 oz. divisions.
5. Trimming knives with spare blades. Hefty handle, 2 off.
6. Coping saw with spare blades.
7. Paring chisel, not sharp.
8. Dreadnought rasps with handles, 4 off.
9. Bricklayer's bolster.
10. 6×3 in. junior G clamps.
11. Screwdrivers, cabinet makers, 6 in., 2 off.
12. Carpenter's claw hammer, $1\frac{1}{4}$ lb.
13. Rubber faced mallet. Not wood or fibre.
14. Stainless steel solid table knives, 2 off.
15. Straight edge, 2 in. $\times$ 1 in. timber, 3 ft. long.
16. Stirring sticks, 15 in. $\times$ 1 in. square scrap wood, 6 off.

17. 4 or 6 plywood slips, 1½ or 3 mm. ply, 3 in. by 12 in. for separating moulds.
18. Clean jam or vegetable tins, 7 lb. size approximately, or 1-gallon polythene jars, 6 off.
19. Supply of polishing cloths.
20. Wetting out board, sheet alloy preferred, 2 ft. by 1 ft., $\frac{1}{16}$ in. thick.
21. Alloy tent pole or scrap TV aerial rod, approximately 5 ft. long, for extension brush.
22. 10 c.c. polythene measuring bottle, for liquid catalyst.
23. Supply of wing nuts and bolts, $\frac{3}{16}$ in. shank diam. one per 2 ft. run of flange.
24. Drill bits to drill holes in flanges allowing clearance for bolt shanks.

CLOTHING

Clothing will become fouled with resin drips and glass scraps, and a general messy appearance results. Resin drips onto the floor where it is picked up on shoes and carried to other parts of the building. Sanding operations release clouds of glass dust into the air, dust which is harmful if breathed into the lungs in any quantity. It settles everywhere and is mostly associated with the making of the first plug and copy moulds. Trimming casts in the moulds, if done at just the right moment, does not raise a dust. Commercial manufacturers use diamond wheels driven by air motors for trimming, and the operators must wear dust masks. Suitable clothing is as follows:

1. Old shoes. If the soles are holed insert a piece of cardboard to protect the feet. The shoes must be comfortable. They soon build up a patina of 'gunge' and the soles quickly thicken with trodden-in resin and glass.
2. Trousers. These should be old but not holed. If worn over decent trousers resin may soak through so it is better to change completely.
3. Overall, coat or boiler suit with sleeves. The whole body should be covered as completely as possible.
4. Hair, if worn long, will require covering.
5. An old towel round neck to absorb sweat.

6. Household gloves or proper lay-up gloves.
Change outside the workshop to avoid fouling good clothes.

It is assumed that one will buy materials in quantities sufficient for six canoes, or units of six, these canoes being about 14 to 15 ft. long, beam 24 in. and with a 3 oz. lay-up. Attempts to buy in lesser quantities will result in a substantial increase in unit cost. Once an account has been established with a firm repeat orders are less difficult. Not many big firms are willing to supply the odd roll of glass or drum of resin, and stockists obviously require their percentage on the materials. It pays, as always, to shop around. I have worked on a unit cost of 25p per pound weight finished but this, even now, is being left behind and a more realistic unit cost would now be 30p per pound weight finished, and that at rock-bottom prices.
Materials required are as follows:

1. Roll of glass mat, $1\frac{1}{2}$ oz., 60 lb. on roll. Type 'A' glass will do.
2. Drums of resin, boat building type, 168 lb. usually sold in 56 lb., 100 lb. or 112 lb. drums.
3. Drums or cans of gelcoat, flexible boat building type, either 10 lb. cans, 56 lb. drums (a saving) or larger sizes. Allow 5 lb. per canoe.
4. Cans of catalyst, 1 lb. a time, paste or liquid, 1/30th by weight of resin ordered. Say 6 lb. for six canoes.
5. Cans of colour; sold by the pound at from 10/- to £1 per pound. About 1/30th by weight of resin ordered. 6 lb. for six canoes.
6. Accelerator (not needed if resin type number is suffixed (PA) meaning pre-accelerated). Sold in 1 or 9 lb. cans. Ask for one 9 lb. can.
7. Release agent. Carnauba wax polish NOT silicone. 7 lb. tin.
8. Release agent number 2, PVA liquid, coloured, 9 lb. bottle.
9. Solvent. This is usually a methylated alcohol with a very low flash point. It should be bought in 5 gal. drums as it costs less that way. It presents a fire risk and should be kept outside in a lockable steel bin. Small quantities, not more than a gallon may be kept indoors. No smoking obviously.

10. 7 lb. tin of barrier cream made specially for GRP workshops. That which the chemist sells is usually grossly over-priced in comparison.

11. 7 lb. tin of hand cleanser for GRP work. It will come from the same supplier.

12. Brushes. These are classed as consumable materials so allow one for each canoe made. Order in lots of one dozen brushes at a time. 2 in. brushes are right. The handles must be unpainted.

13. Rollers; these should be 2 in., in steel, alloy or nylon. 2 or 4 are required.

14. Foaming resin material for pouring in buoyancy blocks in the end of the canoes. Fairly expensive per canoe unless bought in lots of 10 lb. and upwards.

15. Deck line material. Buy in reels of 500 ft. at a time. $\frac{1}{2}$ in. circumference or $\frac{5}{8}$ in. circumference is about right, polypropylene line, laid.

16. Spray deck material. Depending on size of cockpit, allow $1\frac{1}{3}$ yards per deck, and about 9 ft. of elastic shock cord.

TERMS USED

Mould

This is a canoe-shaped shell made from GRP, highly polished on the inside and varying in weight from 60 to 80 lb. for the complete mould. Manufacturers make moulds which may weigh 3 or 4 cwt. and which should make 200 or 300 canoes. Amateurs will probably get 40 to 60 canoes from their moulds with any luck at all; but moulds can be ruined by one mistake.

Mould/jig

This is a set of moulds, usually one part for the deck and one part for the hull which can be fitted together so that the hull edge and the deck edge are held in perfect register until the joint is made. There are many moulds about, usually hull only, but there is a growing number of mould/jigs available and they turn out better jobs more quickly.

Plug

This is the master shape. It may be timber (which is best), cardboard and GRP, plaster, clay, concrete filled with plaster or it may be a cast from the first mould which is highly polished and used for a succession of copy moulds. In the latter case the plug can be converted to a canoe in two hours or less. Once it is a canoe it is not possible to take another mould from it unless a split deck mould is used.

Flange

In order to fasten hull and deck moulds together it is necessary to have a flange which protrudes around the periphery along the line of widest beam. Simple flanges are flat and rely on bolt holes to hold them in register. This method is unsatisfactory because the bolt holes wear and accurate register to 10 thou. is lost.

Keyed flange

In order to overcome the difficulty of loss of register in the flanges, keys are introduced so that when one half mould is placed over the other the keys and corresponding slots cause the flanges to be

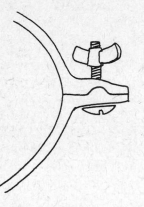

self-aligning. Bolting is then a matter for vertical hold only and may be quite lightly done about every 2 ft. instead of every 8 in. Keyed flanges assist accurate register and quick assembly of mould/jig, taking as much as 30 min. less than the assembly time needed for unkeyed flanges. However, the flanges and keys must be kept very clean.

Lay-up

The lay-up is the method of lamination used. One may have chopped strand glass, woven rovings or cloth lay-up. The lay-up weight is usually stated in the weight per square foot of the glass which goes into the job. 1 oz. chopped strand glass mat weighs 1 oz. per square foot. A 3 oz. lay-up is three layers of 1 oz. mat, or two layers of 1½ oz. mat.

CSM

This is a short name for chopped strand glass mat and consists of a random scatter of strands of glass each about 2 in. long, the whole bound into a mat-like sheet by a binding agent which accepts resin easily thus assisting wetting out. CSM is measured in ounces per square foot.

Woven rovings

This is a sacking like material made of woven strands of glass, each very long, and taking on the finished appearance of a heavy cloth. Rovings are also found on a reel of one single strand, rarely used for canoe building.

Woven rovings are measured in ounces per square yard. 9 oz. woven rovings being the same weight as 1 oz. CSM.

Wetting out

When the resin is brought into contact with the glass the emulsion which binds the strands of glass together accepts the resin and combines with it. The CSM which is quite stiff to handle at first becomes quite limp and soggy after about 2 min. If the glass is not laid before wetting out is complete, it becomes very difficult to lay, as with making the joint. As wetting out takes place air bubbles tend to collect under the glass strands and must be rolled out.

Resin

There are about 180 different kinds of resin, all suitable for different purposes. Always ask for boat building resins for building canoes. Resins with which one builds the moulds are much harder and take a higher polish but most amateurs are satisfied with the less expensive boat building resin for making moulds. The term resin usually refers to the resin used in laminating which is fairly thin and runny and wets the mat easily.

Gelcoat

Gelcoat is a thicker resin, having thixotropic qualities. It is useful for making a surface layer to seal in the glass strands which might otherwise protrude and spoil the finish.

Gunge

A slang term used to indicate rubbish and waste, usually wet and sloppy.

Gunge-bucket

The slop tin in which the brushes receive their first washing out in solvent. The solvent quickly becomes fouled and thick, and if left a few hours in a warm room will set into a jelly.

Curing

The resin must set after the catalyst and accelerator are mixed and the time it takes to set is called the curing time, jelling time or setting time.

BUILDING PROCESS

Mould preparation

1. Chip off flakes of resin, wash moulds, dry.
2. Barrier cream on hands and forearms.
3. Wax polish, once or twice, depending on mould condition.
4. Apply PVA separator, mould release number two. Allow to dry thoroughly. Use a soft plastic sponge.
5. Person in charge checks that all is ready.

Lay-up: stage one

6. Mix gelcoat

Fast	Deck	2 lb.
Fast	Hull	3 lb.
Fast	Cockpit	$\frac{1}{2}$ lb.

7. Brush gelcoat onto moulds as evenly as possible right up to mould flanges.
8. Clean brushes and clean out cans.
9. Gelcoat must set so that finger tip touch no longer brings colour off on finger tip. Raise temperature of mould to 80 deg. F if possible.

Lay-up: stage two

10. Mix lay-up resin

Medium	Deck	4 lb.
Medium	Hull	4 lb.
Slow	Cockpit	2 lb.

11. Paint resin all over mould, especially up to flange, and at once lay in the glass mat and roll down into resin before it drains down into mould bottom. Take first layer within ½ in. of flange edge but *not* protruding above edge.
12. Roll all over to press glass down into resin, especially up to cast edges. Follow up with brushes stippling dry patches.
13. Paint last of first mix of resin into mould and paint in more resin from second 4 lb. mix which should be faster.
14. Lay in second layer of glass, roll down. Leave ½ in. between edge of second lamination and first lamination with no waste above mould edge.
15. Ensure that ends are being laid up with care to ensure that no weakness is found there.
16. Cover side decks beside cockpit with spare pieces.
17. Roll repeatedly to squeeze out air bubbles trapped under glass—they may be heard fizzing out under pressure.
18. Check that all spare is being used, especially resin-splashed pieces which can still be used whilst resin is wet.
19. If 1 oz. mat is being used three layers are usual, but with 1½ oz. material, one must take great care not to waste large spare pieces of glass, having only two layers with which to work.
20. Check all resin dry patches receive extra resin and rolling.
21. Wash out brushes and rollers in solvent. Brushes are then washed out in cleansing cream and hot water. Clean out cans, also.
22. All scraps are put in bin outdoors. Setting resin generates heat which means a fire risk.

Stage two should be completed in 1½ hours with three or four able assistants.

Lay-up: stage three

23. Use chisel, not very sharp, to clean flange of all drips. Anything that may prop flanges apart must be removed.
24. Fix footrest, and loops for equipment anchorage.

25. Wax flanges thickly; take care that none spreads onto cast inner edge.
26. Bolt up top and bottom halves of mould/jig.
27. Sling up on edge, cockpit hole towards light.
28. Have 18 in. strips of glass ready, each 2½ in. wide (approx.) enough to cover whole of joint gap twice over.

Stage four

29. Set out wetting-out board, long handled brush and ordinary brush.
30. Mix 1 lb. lay-up resin, coloured, fast mix.
31. Using long brush, brush resin onto inner face of joint gap, about 2 in. each side of joint line. Work from extreme ends to within arm's reach of cockpit hole.
32. Slop resin onto a strip of glass with short brush and lay it *at once* onto long brush and carry it into mould so that the brush may be turned over to drop pre-wetted strip into place. This *must* be done at once (within a minute) before the resin wets out the strip and it becomes soggy and unmanageable. The strip covers the joint and seals it from the inside. It must span the space between opposite laminations.

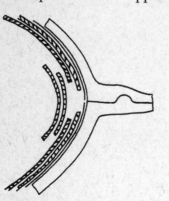

Sealing the joint

33. The strips settle onto the joint without further help. Note that any internal obstruction will lift strips away from surface to which they should adhere and cause a faulty joint. The joint receives two layers of strips, 1½ oz. each.
34. Once the joint has been made to within arm's reach of the hole continue with jointing with short brush and normal hand

laminating system on the job. Pre-wetting is not necessary where direct pressure may be applied. Always leave the joint near the hole until last. See notes.

35. Clean brushes and cans.
36. Ensure that resin gels so that, when job is turned over to do the other side, the resin wet strips will not fall off the higher side. If this does happen, strip out faulty pieces and do again.
37. Turn whole job over and do the other side. Leave undisturbed for 24 hours.

Stage five

38. Remove all nuts and bolts.
39. Batter outside of mould gently with side of clenched fist. See air slip between cast and mould.
40. Lever flanges apart with bolster and prop open with wooden blocks.
41. Beat mould with clenched fist until two halves spring apart. Cast will be still fixed in one half.
42. Separate the other half by bending flanges downwards and inserting ply slips between cast and mould. Work around and then beat ends of mould flange down so that cast pops up at one or other end. Lift out.
43. Moulds now ready to start at (1) again. Trim casting flash from cast.

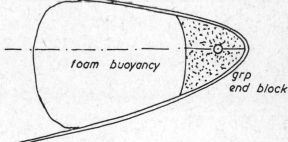

Finishing. End blocks and buoyancy blocks

44. Stand canoe on end and lash upright.
45. Seal outer edges of joint, from lower end upwards along joint about 6 in., with 'sausages' of clay or strips of masking tape.
46. Mix ¼ lb. of resin, fast mix, puddle in some glass scraps, and pour into lower end of canoe.

47. Allow to set. When heat is being produced mix two-part foaming resin buoyancy material and pour into lower end. The exotherm of the end block setting will initiate rapid bubbling and setting of foaming resin. Ensure sides of canoe are warmed, to about 80 deg. F. A cold canoe will result in a shrivelled block of foaming resin.
48. Turn end for end and repeat.

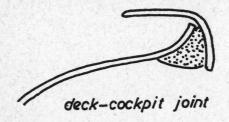

deck-cockpit joint

Finishing: seat

49. Take finished seat, all edges smoothed, and place it into hole in deck. Cockpit mould and deck mould must be matched.
50. Tie into place with cord with small loop at one end so that really firm tension may be applied to lashing. Ensure seat and rim sit tightly into hole rim. Use small G clamps to hold down ends of rim.
51. Sling up almost completely upside down but with one side of cockpit rim slightly higher than the other. The job should be at shoulder height.
52. Mix ¼ lb. of resin, fast mix, with about three times as much chalk by volume, and stir into a stiff paste. It should be putty-like in consistency.
53. Use table knife to trowel paste into crack between seat and deck, starting at the difficult bit behind the hip flanges. Do the other side of the cockpit behind the difficult place before doing the easy parts. The finger makes a good jointing tool being more flexible and sensitive than the table knife. Clean excess resin away from under rim flange by wiping out with finger tip. If insufficient chalk has been used, the resin will bulge out of the joint and drip away.
54. Allow to set and trim off lumps and rough edges with chisel whilst 'green'.

Note. The whole of the weight of the paddler is taken by the cockpit rim joint and the paddler may be in contact with the seat for several hours at a time, so it must be comfortable with no rough edges.

NOTES

THESE NOTES REFER TO PRACTICE IN 1968. NOW, IN 1972, MUCH QUICKER, MORE PROFESSIONAL METHODS PRODUCE CANOES WEIGHING ABOUT 30 LBS. FIRMS SUPPLYING THE MATERIALS ALSO SUPPLY UP-TO-DATE ADVICE, BUT BASICALLY THE METHODS REMAIN THE SAME.

Numbers refer to numbers of directions under 'Building Process'.
2
Barrier cream must be used. Some, a very few, will develop dermatitis when resinous chemicals touch the skin. Most people will experience itchiness, usually of the soft skin on the inside of the wrists. This should stop as soon as the cleansing cream is used and the hands are thoroughly washed. If itchiness and redness of the skin persists for a day or two after using the resins see your doctor and ask his advice, which may be to leave the materials severely alone. It is possible to handle the materials for some time and develop sensitivity later. One member of a group developed signs of dermatitis but it turned out that he had been cleaning a car engine with diesel oil and this had apparently caused the incipient dermatitis.
6, 10, 13, 30, 46, 52
Mixing resin should be done with thought for the time available for completion of the job, the nature of the job and the stage reached in the job.
Time sense: one must trim the cockpit hole edge at some stage, so it is wise to make the first mix of 4 lb. for the deck lamination about medium setting rate so that it will be gelled about $1\frac{1}{2}$ hours after beginning. The second mix which is necessary after about $\frac{3}{4}$ hour should be a fast mix so that it will catch up with the first mix setting rate by the end of the laminating time, thus leaving a waste edge of equal stiffness to be trimmed. If a fast mix is used at both stages the trimming will be difficult because the first mix will have set hard and the second will be too wet and sloppy. Attempts to slice the waste away will result in de-lamination of the later layers. A hard-set waste edge must be sawn off.
A slow job, such as making a seat cast, will require a slow mix

otherwise one will be still working and the resin will be setting before it can be used.

A really fast mix is required for jobs such as joining up, which must be done quickly if they are to be right. If they take too much time you can guarantee that they will be faulty. The fast mix is to allow one to turn the job over and complete the other side of the hull joint in the same session. One person should be able to do all the joining up in an hour.

The rate at which one's team normally works should be considered when laying up. Skill and experience will allow a shortening of the time required for resin setting.

Two kinds of resin are supplied: pre-accelerated and non accelerated. PA resin may be very quick to set and the setting rate is adjusted by the addition of the necessary amount (but never less than 2 per cent by weight) of catalyst. Non PA is adjusted for setting rate by the addition of more or less accelerator. No accelerator will result in a setting time of up to two or three days in cold air. Too much accelerator will actually inhibit setting. The maximum amount one should add is about 10 to 15 c.c. of accelerator per pound of resin. The table gives mixing recommendations.

Room temperature	65 deg. F	70 deg. F	80 deg. F
Mixture speed Slow 1–2 hours	3–6 c.c.	2–4 c.c.	1–2 c.c.
Medium $\frac{1}{2}$–1 hour	6–10 c.c.	4–8 c.c.	2–4 c.c.
Fast $\frac{1}{4}$–$\frac{1}{2}$ hour	10–15 c.c.	8–12 c.c.	4–8 c.c.

The quantities given are the number of cubic centimetres of accelerator to be added to each pound of resin used in the job. Further points to be remembered when handling resins are:

Catalyst is obtained as a paste or a liquid. The liquid may splash and cause severe burning of soft tissues and irritation of tougher parts. It must be washed off at once. Splashed eyes may be bathed in a 2 per cent aqueous solution of sodium bicarbonate. Paste catalyst may be wiped onto face by contaminated hand as when brushing sweat away from eyes but cannot splash.

Catalyst and accelerator should not be mixed directly together; always mix catalyst into resin before adding accelerator. Mixing the liquid catalyst and accelerator in sufficiently large quantities may result in explosive decomposition of the catalyst which is an unstable organic peroxide.

Colour paste should be dispersed in a little resin before mixing the pre-coloured resin into the bulk of the resin. The colour should be mixed in before the catalyst and accelerator are added. Colour pastes will inhibit setting rates to a greater or lesser degree.

If large quantities of catalyst are stored on the premises the local fire officer must be informed as burning catalyst is a very dangerous hazard requiring special treatment.

One last point about safety precautions: these notes are for guidance only and are not all that one requires for a full knowledge of GRP work. You are advised most earnestly to read the books listed at the end of the chapter.

21

Washing out brushes and rollers is important. With rollers it is enough to brush the rollers in a can of solvent and leave for a short while before shaking out and standing to dry. If resin and glass are allowed to set between the rollers about the only way of cleaning is to fire them, which will not do for plastic rollers. During use, after an hour or so, the roller may be found to be dragging the glass laminations. This is the result of resin setting on the spindle and causing the discs to drag. A quick soak in solvent puts that right.

The brushes should be washed out in the 'gunge bucket' in the most contaminated solvent first and then in a can of clean solvent. They are then shaken to remove the solvent, rubbed in hand cleaner and rubbed over the hands, thus cleaning hands and brush at the same time. It is necessary to work the bristles between the fingers in order to free the thickening resin trapped at the roots of the bristles. This resin when set will drop out onto the job and cause delamination where it rests between two layers. Alternatively, the resin builds up in a block and makes the brush solid and unusable. Never leave the rollers or the brushes in the solvent for more than an hour or so. It is easy to forget them so that, within two or three days, the whole mass of contaminated solvent and brush or roller is congealed into a jellylike lump. Brushes with jellyfied solvent trapped in the bristles may be cleaned to some extent by beating with a hammer on a piece of wood and then soaking in clean solvent or even paint remover. Any brush which has become hard should be thrown away.

22

Resin whilst setting generates heat. This is the 'exotherm' which may ignite paper scraps in the bin into which scraps are dropped.

31

It is a good plan to leave the easy part of the job to last so that, in the event of the resin for the joint setting rapidly, it may be used quickly on the easy part of the joint in a few minutes. Remember that resin in bulk sets quicker than resin spread out onto the job.

39

The air will be seen to slip between the mould and the cast only if the mould is a translucent uncoloured resin. A coloured mould prevents this being seen although it is possible to hear the air penetrating—a thump with a fist on the mould makes a cracking sort of knock when air moves compared with a dull thud if no air moves. Do not strike with heavy blows.

47

Foaming resin is made up from two parts which are mixed in equal quantities in a mixing jar. ½ lb. of each part is about right for either end of the canoe for buoyancy purposes. The mixing must be done within half a minute as foaming begins almost at once—certainly within a minute.

52

Many people will not use chalk as it adds bulk and weight and detracts from strength. The joint may be made with slips of pre-wetted mat as an alternative.

DETAILS

Footrest

A solid footrest is necessary for safety and ease of handling in rough water and for power from the drive on the paddles. While surfing one may be travelling at around 15 m.p.h. when the nose may dip under the face of the wave and a loop result. If, while dipping, the bows strike bottom a solid impact is felt which may

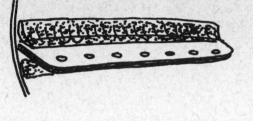

Footrests

smash even a strong footrest. The footrest may be required to stand the impact of 180 lb. travelling at 22 ft. per second; the impact energy is enormous. Few footrests are strong enough for that sort of energy absorption.

Two plates are prepared, each about 12 in. long by about 3 in. wide and tapered to allow for the inward sweep of the bows. The inner edges of the flanges must be parallel. The two prepared flanges are clamped to a jig, which itself is clamped to the mould flanges after lamination and before the joint is made. The flanges are adjusted so that they will be set into place at the right distance from the cockpit hole when it is eventually assembled. Glass and resin is laid along the joint between flanges and hull interior. A 3 or 4 oz. lay-up should do. The flanges should be about $1\frac{1}{2}$ in. below the joint line to allow the joint to be made. The flanges are jig-drilled and a heavy alloy cross bar is fixed with nuts and bolts.

Loops

It is usually difficult to tie equipment into a GRP canoe as the inside is smooth and without points to which lashings may be made. Make cord 'grommets' about 2½ in. diameter, and resin-and-glass them at one point of the loop to the bottom of the canoe, or, better still, to the sides just below the joint line. It is then easy to tie equipment to the loops. Framed canoes are well supplied with tieing points.

Deck lines

The ends of the canoe when plugged with resin blocks are ready for drilling. A ¼ in. or ⅜ in. drill will make a hole of suitable size right through the resin block. Drill through the hull on the joint line about 1½ in. back from the extreme ends of the canoe. The edges of the hole should be chamfered. Those who require a more workmanlike job may care to drill through the ends *before* the end blocks are cast and put in a metal tube with belled ends. The resin then moulds itself around the tube inside the canoe making a strong and well finished job.

The tubes or holes are then used as anchorage points for the end loops. The loop should be big enough to go through the hole and then be spliced back or made into a grommet. A large loop into which one may put the whole hand is required by ICF regulations.

Court and Goodwin, C2 event. Note end loop on bows. ICF regulations require that these cords shall have a minimum diameter of 6 mm. Wide grasp on paddle shaft gives greater control and 'low geared' power, but less speed.

The deck lines are fixed through the end loops and to fixing points level with the front of the cockpit on the deck. The lines should be strong synthetic fibre cord, at least $\frac{1}{2}$ in. circumference. (ICF Competition Rules specify 6mm. diameter cord.)

Stiffeners

Before the two halves are joined it is possible to lay in stiffeners. These should lie along the length of the canoe in the hull but may run across the deck as stiffening beams, i.e. just in front of and behind the cockpit. An effective stiffener will be about 1 in. high and about 1 in. across its base with a 'top hat' section. Two layers of mat are sufficient strength for it. Its shape may be set by a very light, $1\frac{1}{2}$ oz., cast in a special mould, the cast being moulded into the canoe after the last lamination has been laid. Alternatively, a piece of rolled corrugated cardboard will do the job when overlaid with two layers of pre-wetted $1\frac{1}{2}$ oz. glass mat. Paper rope often has a wire core which permits it to be shaped and laid accurately into position. Corrugated cardboard is the least expensive and easiest method. The strength of the stiffener is in its section shape. A deck may be reduced in lay-up weight by using only two layers of 1 oz. CSM instead of three provided stiffeners are moulded in.

The following timetables were originally drawn up for a school group but may be adapted for use by any group.

SPECIMEN TIMETABLE: MOULD COPYING (ONE WEEKEND)

Friday evening	Ensure that the workshop is prepared and every-thing is ready.
Saturday	
09.00	Group assembles. Five or six people per mould.
09.30	Wash moulds and plugs, polish, separate, including seat.
10.30	Mix and apply gelcoat, leave to set.
11.00	Start laminating first half of mould and seat mould.
13.00	Finish laminating.
	LUNCH
16.00	Turn over, separate and lift off original half mould.

16.30	Wash off mould, polish, separate.
18.00	Mix and apply gelcoat.
19.00	Start laminating.
21.00	Finish laminating.
21.30	Clean up.
22.00	Disperse.

Sunday

10.00	Group re-assembles. Only two or three people are now essential.
10.30	Trim flanges, drill flanges, separate.
11.00	Moulds separated, finishing touches, painting on name and number and date of job.
11.30	All tools cleaned and set aside, original plug and mould cleaned up ready for taking home.
12.00	Disperse.

SPECIMEN TIMETABLE: CANOE BUILDING (TWO WEEKS)

Wednesday	Evening. Wash out moulds leave to dry.
Thursday	Midday. Polish moulds, separate, leave to dry.
Friday	Midday. Mix and apply gelcoat.
	Evening. Lay-up session, six people, two hours. Stay until casts set ready for trimming. Should finish about 7.00 p.m. Now there are two casts in moulds, deck and hull, and cockpit on mould.
Monday	Take off cockpit cast and clean up. Bolt up mould-jig for canoe shell.
Tuesday	Midday. Lay one side of hull-deck joint, 45 min.
	Evening. Lay other side of joint. Leave in moulds.
Wednesday	Separate moulds, wash and begin again.
Thursday	Evening. Put cockpit into deck, seal in.
Monday	Midday. Run in one end plug and buoyancy.
	Evening. Run in other end plug and buoyancy.
Tuesday	Drill ends with rigging holes, form end loops and run deck lines.
Wednesday	Fit on spray deck and launch.

This method has been applied at several schools, both boys and girls, and after a delay of two weeks turns out one canoe per week.

FURTHER READING

If one wants to go more thoroughly into GRP canoe building methods then it would pay to read the books listed underneath.

Technical Manual No. 12, British Resin Products, Devonshire House, Piccadilly, London W1.

Polyester Handbook, Scott-Bader & Co Ltd, Wollaston, Wellingborough, Northants.

Trade magazine, *Reinforced Plastics*, Craftsman Publications, 18 Dufferin Street, London EC1. Subscription only.

Building a GRP Canoe, "Streamlyte", Lancing, Sussex.

"Trylon", Thrift Street, Woolaston, Wellingborough, Northants, publish a canoe-building booklet of which I am joint author and which is really up-to-date at the time of this revision.

Since this book was first published, I have prepared a further book for A & C Black, *Canoe Building in GRP*. Four years of concentrated effort in the Riverside workshops to build canoes and to bring into use new designs, have produced much more detailed information, a knowledge of tools and techniques used in the motor-body finishing trade which are indispensable to canoe builders, and a re-assessment of basic attitudes. For example, one important conclusion I have reached in the time is that when one first experiences canoeing, the first influence is the sight of the canoe, therefore it must be a pleasing colour, have a brilliant polish with true glittering highlights, and it must have a pleasing shape. Next, the novice carries the canoe to the water, so it must be as light as possible consonant with sufficient strength for its purpose, and finally it must handle well.

Chapter 16

Storage and Transport
of Canoes and Equipment

With the introduction of GRP canoes, methods of storing and carrying canoes have altered: more is now possible. Most people must carry their canoes to the water and manufacturers now make trailers to carry canoes; some do it effectively and others less effectively.

Many canoes have been carried for many miles on the roof of my car and most of the faults possible have been experienced and dealt with. I now make it a firm rule to tie canoes on my car roof personally.

Roof rack

The car roof requires some protection as well as the canoe. Much depends on the roof construction as to whether it will carry the loads imposed. Where the two flanges meet at the gutter edge is the best place to take the load on the roof. Racks with rubber feet, even twin feet, will press down into the thin roof material and ruin its shape. Also, as the weight of the load enlarges the depression under the feet, the tension on the securing hooks relaxes and the rack is then free to take off complete with load.

The shallow basket type of rack is rarely any good for carrying canoes but the dinghy-carrying type is usually excellent. However, the twin rail or ladder rack often has raised supports which come above the top level of the rail and grind holes in the hull of a GRP canoe on a long trip unless well padded.

Recently I prepared the roof of my car for casting resin and glass onto it. Using two layers of 2 oz. glass, I completely covered the roof from gutter to gutter and from front to back. Unfortunately, the edge of the casting locked dovetail fashion into the gutter and it was necessary to break it out and patch the pieces of cast together later in the workshop. Having made the GRP 'wig', I braced the large and floppy moulding on a workbench and laid across the roof at either end two cardboard 'top hat' section rails running from side to side. Pre-wetted glass pieces were laid over this and box-section stiffeners were built up from three layers of 2 oz. mat. The whole was then quite stiff. It weighed about 18 lb. and cost about £3 to make. Alloy tubes, sections from old tent

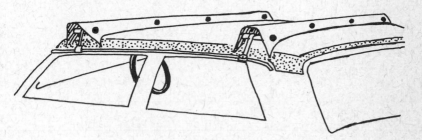

Do-it-yourself roofrack

pole material, were pushed into holes on the outer extension of the cross rails and these made attachment points for the gutter hooks which hold the rack down. To protect the roof a ½ in. thick foam plastic liner was fitted between car roof and false roof. The false roof gives heat insulation, roof protection, spreads the load and carries canoes most effectively. The main difficulty is that one must make it for oneself as no commercial outfit is available to my knowledge. It took me about two whole days to make.

Provided that one remembers that it is necessary to spread the imposed load across the whole of the roof, preferably to the gutters, then many alternative methods for carrying become possible. A partially inflated car inner tube will take the centre of the canoe and, as it spreads out, will transfer the imposed load to a wide ring shaped area of the roof which may spring inwards.

The tube should not be so hard as to restrict the area of contact with the roof nor so soft that the canoe bounces and scuffs on the roof. The lashing system is most important with this method. The overhanging bow and stern must be located by inverted V lashings to the front and rear bumper bars. The front end of the canoe must be restricted by a rope from the rear bumper bar to the front of the canoe so that it will not lunge over onto the bonnet under heavy braking. A camping foam-plastic mattress is very good for locating the canoe in a soft, supporting, non-slip pad.

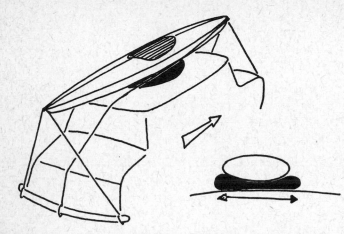

"Inner tube" roof rack

These methods of spreading the load are first-class on a dry roof but in heavy rain the area of contact between rubber and roof becomes very slippery. In this case it is better to take a further lashing round the load and through the car windows to make a loop which locates the load and stops lateral displacement. Unfortunately, this also prevents the ready opening of rear doors.

Special racks

A commercial roof rack, made by a firm of canoeing enthusiasts, consists of a rail, about 7 ft. long, of rectangular section steel tube with V or U shaped brackets firmly welded to each end. This rack is clamped to the ladder rack cross rails by inverted U bolts and the V section brackets carry a strong strop from tip to tip which form a flexible cradle for the canoe. The canoe is held down by rubber shock cords. This is a most popular method and very secure. It does, of course, reduce the clearance available for entering low garages, but it is quickly dismantled.

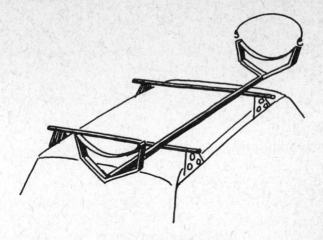

Commercial roof rack

Knots and lashings

Certain knots give better results than others. Some people tie knot after knot on a piece of cord to shorten it, which is unnecessary. The knots I use are bowline, upholsterers knot, round turn and two half hitches; these will tie any canoe to any car roof. When tying a canoe down to a roof rack it is often not possible to make the cord very tight. It is also frequently the case that, after a few miles of motoring, the lashings ease off and the canoe starts to wander about the roof. Synthetic cords do not alter length according to their state of wetness or dryness as do natural fibres. Natural fibre cords, when used wet to tie down a canoe, will dry out unless there is rain and slacken off very rapidly as one is driving along. In order to take up the slack quickly it is useful to have a tensioner in the knotting system which can be approached from the near (the less hazardous) side of the car.

A lightweight canoe, say 30 lb. and under, will spend most of its time while travelling floating on the cushion of high speed air blasting upwards off the sloping windscreen. This floating effect begins about 40 m.p.h. when the canoe is to be seen weaving about quite gently, held down by its lashings but clear of the roof bearers. Really, provided the speed is moderate and not so great that violent turbulence and eddies cause the canoe to buck and jump at its cords, this is a good place for the canoe to be as it almost eliminates scuffing of the hull of the canoe against the roof bearers. If one usually drives at just about that critical speed at which lift begins then a great deal of scuffing will take place. In this case it is better to lash the canoe down tightly on to padded bearers. However, it is possible to make the lashings so firm that as one sets off, and vibration begins, the canoe hull suddenly buckles and collapses a little, allowing the lashings to slacken. A GRP hull would not suffer great harm as a result of a short trip in a buckled condition but, on a long trip, might develop fatigue fractures at the point of maximum flexion of the hull.

If one is travelling at high speeds on a motorway with a canoe up, it is almost impossible to eliminate shudder and bucking of the canoe, unless the lashings are so tight that the canoe shell buckles. In this case, I fly my canoe quite happily under its lashings but put an extra lashing at its nose to hold it in proper relationship with the front of the car. An inverted V lashing, knotted at the nose of the canoe as well, to prevent wander of the nose on a slipping loop, provides this stability of entry into the air and the hull will then trail like a wind sock.

In high side winds one must be absolutely certain that the roof rack is reliable. Launching twin canoes at 70 m.p.h. into a fast moving traffic stream could have the most appalling consequences. Remember that it is possible for the roof rack to slacken its clamps when in use though appearing quite tight when the load is off. Lashing the ends down firmly with cords may take enough tension from the clamps for them to slacken and slip; thus, whilst the canoe may be secure endways, it may lack holding power laterally and a side wind will lift it and rip it from its moorings.

The cords *must* be first-class. Clothes-line simply *will not do*. I use and replace each year, a polypropylene line of $\frac{5}{8}$ in. circumference; laid cord as distinct from woven cord. I prefer laid cord as I can splice it easily. The cord is made up into lengths about 16 ft. long. They can then double in emergency as deck lines for canoes up to 15 ft. long. Cords longer than that will lead to lashings which owe more to patience than ingenuity. Also, I find that classes of novices may be introduced to knots if handy lengths of cord are available to play with. To save on the cost of these cords I buy a reel of 500 ft. of cord direct from the manufacturers, who will usually supply single reels by return.

Method of lashing

When loading up two canoes on my car roof (see p. 197), I lay one in position on the offside of the roof. Two cords are used, one fore and one aft. One end is tied to the rack with a bowline or an upholsterer's knot which is not adjustable. The cord passes over the canoe and is looped through a hole in the cross piece. It is then looped in a round turn about the shafts of the two paddles which lie between the two canoes and then looped through the hole in the cross piece on the other side of the middle of the roof. From there it goes up over the second canoe, which is loaded on after the paddles have been placed, and the cords are all tightened up. The ends of the cords then come down to their respective lashing points and a round turn and two half hitches are used to tie down. This lashing is not very tight but the spare ends of the cords are just long enough to run to the cord at the other end of the roof and to loop in a round turn about it. As tension is applied the cords are pulled together, thus tightening the whole assembly. It is useful to rock the canoes a little whilst doing this to allow the cords to settle into a natural line and to even the tension throughout the cord. The ends of the cords are then tied in two half hitches. The tension adjustment is on the nearside of the car; in streaming wet weather on dark nights by the roadside it is better to be on the sheltered side of the car when making adjustments to the lashings.

TRAILERS

If one wishes to carry four or more canoes a car roof is too small and a trailer is indicated. There are many trailers; home made, commercial, good, bad, legal, illegal, too heavy and too light. The law relating to the construction and use of motor vehicles affects trailers and should be consulted for authoritative guidance. One should bear in mind a number of points in order to have safe and satisfactory motoring with a trailer hitched behind.

Frame

The trailer is not a stationary frame with wheels on it. A canoe rack with cross bars on the cantilever system is fine for ease of storage in a shed but it will fracture its cross bars under normal trailing usage; this will usually be at night, a long way from home and miles from the nearest garage. The knowledge that steel tubes have weight and that joints are subjected to flexing even on an unloaded frame should remind one of the basic and very sound engineering principle that the triangle is a self-supporting and completely rigid structure and a good one to apply to trailer design.

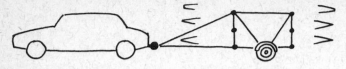

Trailer frame

The load of the frame and its contents should be taken direct to the suspension units and not to the cross beam which carries the units. This is why most dinghy trailers are quite unsuitable for the carrying of canoes. The front of the trailer must always tend to be heavy; this is known as the nose loading or hitch load. It should be about two to four stones for the average canoe trailer, loaded or not. The addition of load to the trailer will, if the centre of gravity is moved substantially, change the handling of the trailer and the towing vehicle.

The frame should be built so that the centre of gravity of the empty framework is about 6 to 8 in. in front of the line joining the wheel centres. The cross bearers should be about 5 or 6 ft. apart, not more, to allow for the shorter baths type of canoes now being used. Of course, if the canoes are normally to be, say, K2s, each about 22 ft. long, then the frame should be about 11 ft. from bearer to bearer. The distance from the centre of gravity to towing hitch of the whole structure should be 18 in. more than half the length of the longest canoe to be carried. If the canoes are the usual solo type of canoe (24 in. by 12 in. at their bulkiest section) then the inner part of the frame should be measured in multiples of 2 ft. if the canoes are carried horizontal, or 1 ft. if carried on edge.

The frame should be light, strong and simple. If the frame and suspension units together weigh more than 2 cwt. unladen then the trailer must have wheel brakes which add about £15 at once to the cost. Rectangular steel tubes which are obtainable on a cost-per-pound weight or cost-per-foot basis are usually obtainable from steel stockists though not all stockists carry the small sizes required. The section should be about 1 in. by 2 in. and either 10 or 12 gauge. Some kinds of steel are easier to weld than others. One should obtain welding quality mild steel.

The suspension should be independent. There are a number of systems available, but I have found the rubber block in torsion unit, about 1,000 lb. capacity per pair, with trailing arm, to be ideal. Steel spring units may be very good, especially the coiled spring type, but they seem to be bulky, heavy and complicated to attach. The rubber-in-torsion unit is mounted on a flat steel plate which is very easy to fix to a framework with six or eight bolts. There is another advantage of the rubber unit in that it is self damping, requiring no additional shock absorbing unit, and it does not require any greasing whatever. The wheel bearings will, of course, require greasing to keep out water.

The lighting system must include rear red lights, each placed not less than 11 in. in from the outermost edge of the trailer frame and load. The number plate must be illuminated. Flashing indicators are required. If the outer edges of the trailer are wider than the towing vehicle by more than 11 in., then forward facing white lights are required. Most trailers are 6 ft. wide and so, the average car being between 5 and 6 ft. wide, white forward facing lights are not usually required. If the load overhangs the vehicle by much more than 3 ft. fore and aft it would be better to hang a red light on the rear of the extended load but the law is a little vague on this matter of overhanging loads where boats are concerned. Theoretically, and some say it has been done, it may be legal to carry 36 ft. of K4 racing kayak on a Mini roof through London without any additional lighting. For the protection of the load and my peace of mind I would indicate the extent of the load by lighting or by a rag tied on securely and fluttering in the wind. It must be very disconcerting to be driving a lorry, say, and to run up close behind the vehicle in front, as some buses do, and find a slim, almost invisible, pointed kayak tapping on the windscreen —or through it. Proper burden boards are used by heavy transport and dimensions and colours for side and end boards are detailed in the regulations.

The towing hitch to the vehicle could be a simple pin but a 50 mm ball hitch is better. It is relatively inexpensive and fits the International Standard for towing hitches. It is much easier to drop the hitch on or lift it off; a standard lighting socket and plug fitted to the vehicle is a good thing to have for ease of hitching up. Twisting straggly wires are messy, unsatisfactory and probably illegal in use.

Whilst working recently with an education authority which uses canoes and "Mirror" class dinghies it became clear that their trailer would carry three "Mirror" dinghies or twelve canoes or some combination with ease. The layout of the trailer and its dimensions are shown below and opposite.

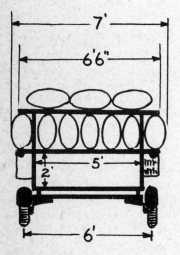

Multi-canoe trailer

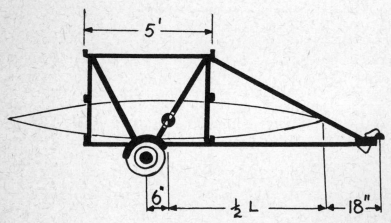

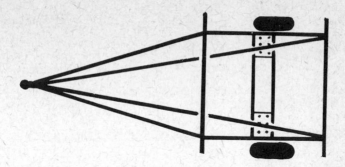

The drawings are the result of many years of experience with trailers, good and bad, and do result in what is as close to the ideal as any trailer for canoes can be. More expensive and heavier trailers are available, but for my money this is the best compromise.

CANOE RACKS

The ideal system for twelve canoes would be to build a garage for the trailer so that it could be wheeled in loaded and use it as a canoe storage rack. A subsidiary racking system would hold the less-used canoes. GRP canoes stand on end quite happily and thus may take up a ground area not more than 2 ft. by 1 ft. Such canoes could be lashed upright to the side of a building with no external covering. The beauty of GRP is that it is almost rot proof and will take treatment that would ruin a canvas covered canoe in a few months. Pigeonhole systems (A) into which one slides canoes at one end may damage canvas covered canoes but are quite satisfactory for GRP canoes. Plywood canoes come somewhere between these two types for durability. If the forward bearer has a free-turning roller built on to it (say an old wringer roller), it will accept canvas canoes without damaging them.

The distance between the rack bearers should be half the length of the canoe. A 15 ft. canoe should be supported on two bearers 7 to 8 ft. apart; the distance is not critical. There should be a clear height of 15 in. between the top of one bearer and the bottom of the next one up. Canoes are probably best supported on a stationary rack which has cantilever bearers to take canoes from

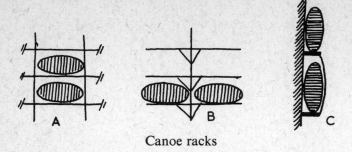

Canoe racks

the side so that the canoe may be lifted gently on to its rack and lowered down (B). If wider gangways are required, as for example in a long passageway, then they will lie quite happily on edge (C), so that the clearance for each canoe is about 2 ft. 3 in. vertically. for a 24 in. wide canoe. The bearers need not protrude more than 8 in. from the wall. Such a system will require cords for fastening each canoe in place. Remember to allow for the curve of the lower canoe when calculating ground clearance. With bearers about 7 ft. apart it should not require more than 3 in. clearance.

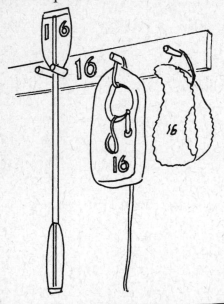

Equipment rack

Equipment racks

Paddles, lifejackets and spray decks should all be racked together and numbered so that losses are at once noted. A standard cockpit opening used by, say, an education authority will require standard spray decks and this is a big advantage in a school or outdoor activity centre. The canoes may be quite different but make the cockpit rims standard even if the seats vary in shape and size.

Paddles can hang vertically from a rack about 7 ft. from the ground, from stubs of plastic water pipe, say 6 in. long, pushed tight into holes drilled in a horizontal board fixed to the wall. The board should be about 5 in. by 1 in. and whatever length is required. Each set of equipment takes 6 in. for the paddle, 12 in. for the lifejacket and a few inches for the spray deck. If each is numbered and hung on its numbered peg gear checks are easy and the condition of individual lifejackets and spray decks may be noted at a glance. Large numerals stencilled or painted on lifejacket fronts also assist ready identification of students on the water. The drawing shows a suitable layout which can be put up in a couple of hours. Damage will occur to gear which is allowed to lie about on the floor. Even in a private house I would prefer to see canoeing equipment properly racked.

Chapter 17

Packing a Canoe

One part of the British Canoe Union test of proficiency is to pack the canoe as for a journey of several days and use it in its loaded condition. Certainly a loaded canoe is rather different in its handling characteristics from an unloaded canoe; however, my type of canoeing depends almost always on a fixed camp site, a car to carry the load and a lightly loaded canoe which is light, lively and a joy to handle in rough water. A heavy canoe should avoid really rough water where violent changes of direction may break paddle or paddler.

The test, which now has the name of the Inland Kayak Proficiency Certificate test, is based on one which the Canoe Camping Club originated and which, naturally, was relevant to their kind of canoeing and camping requirements. It was based on large canoes, by present standards, and they had to carry loads of camping equipment. The really violent stresses which the modern GRP canoe experiences in surf, for instance, would probably destroy a larger, canvas covered canoe. However, many people attend for testing with a modern GRP canoe, possibly of the slalom type with supported deck and small pointed hull. When the bulk of the under deck supporting/buoyancy block has been allowed for there is very little room for camping equipment.

RIVER CANOEING

When camping by canoe one requires tent, sleeping bag, clothing, food, kitchen equipment, small items, first aid kit, canoe repair kit and waterproof bags in which to carry equipment.

Tent
This may be anything from a sheet of polythene and some stakes

to a two- or three-man affair with flysheet and full equipment. I use a Black's Tinker with flysheet; it weighs several pounds, is very weather-worthy and packs into a waterproof bag 7 in. in diameter and 2 ft. long.

Sleeping bag

This should always be better than you can really afford. It may hurt to pay a great deal of money for a first-class sleeping bag but it hurts a lot more to have a sleepless night, stiff with fatigue and cold. I use an Icelandic Special and even that is not enough on really cold nights. I find that it is necessary to have much more under me than over. The fine down filling of the bag is crushed flat under the body and heat loss is very noticeable. An air mattress is better than nothing and a foam camping mattress is more durable but very bulky (packed into a waterproof bag it makes an excellent buoyancy bag having bulk with little weight).

Clothing

My ideal canoeing clothing must be all-weather and unaffected by wet. I would carry, in addition, slacks, a good polo-neck sweater, shoes or good plimsolls and a full change of clothes suitable for a visit to the local inn.

Food and water

I take as little as possible. I prefer to drift off to a local village and buy my fish and chips, pie and a pint or five course dinner as the fancy and the cash takes me. Money is much more transportable than bulky food. I do carry a Horlicks Two-Man emergency pack, bars of chocolate and cans of fruit drinks. If I carry bulky food it is enough for a day or, at the most, two and is usually in the car. Water is carried in a 4 pint screw-top plastic container.

Kitchen equipment

A stove is essential. I find that the little camping gas stoves whilst being handy are very slow to cook food and a good paraffin pressure stove is better. Take a knife, fork and spoon set of the clip-together variety—I never did see the need for a great scout knife strapped to the belt.

The mug can be the metal kind, half-pint size. Plastic is nasty, I find and pottery mugs break easily. Some people carry a few dozen plastic cups, of the disposable type, with a holder.

Also useful are a set of metal dixies—ex-army preferably. The kind I use are ex-US stainless steel; one half becomes an oval frying pan the other half a dish with pressed sections in it. The knife, fork and spoon set conveniently pack into it. The British rectangular dixies hold more but I don't like them so well.

Don't forget matches in a tin (proofed against the wet). Have at least three lots of matches all packed in different places in the canoe. As for tin openers, I prefer the type with a toothed wheel and cutting blade. This wheels around the rim of the can and shears off the lid very neatly.

The real 'lightweight' enthusiast carries a large roll of aluminium foil as used in kitchens, shaping his own disposable cooking pots, plates and cups from that. I never have but it seems like a really good idea; it weighs very little and has little bulk.

Small items

These are partly safety equipment, partly for comfort. I take a three-cell lamp with extension headlight (useful for seeing with when navigating cow pastures on a wet and misty night, signalling for help from off-shore islands or canoeing in dark sea caves).

I always have a compass and a whistle, both plastic, tied to lanyards so I don't lose them when in deep waters.

A can opener of the type used for piercing beer cans is useful.

A 'Miniflare' pack, for which one now requires a firearms certificate, costs £2 for the certificate for three years and £4 for the flares. (Rarely of use inland.)

A length of polypropylene laid cord is needed as a heaving line, for binding things up or whatever. It should be about 50 ft. long and not less than $\frac{1}{2}$ in. circumference. A short length of cord for practising knots is a useful aid to conversation in the early part of an evening before the talking begins.

Car keys should be tied to a lanyard or pinned inside the anorak pouch and money in a screw topped film can.

Sun glasses are a must especially on open waters. The glare that reflects from sea or lake even on a dull day can strain the eyes.

Toilet requisites are soap, razor, toothbrush, army ration pack soap for lathering in sea water, towel, toilet paper.

Take a little trowel or a heavy knife for digging holes.

Nikonos make an all weather camera which is pressure proofed for underwater use and although it is expensive, it takes very good photographs with its wide angle lens. Sand, water, dust—none of these bother it.

First aid

Burn dressings, strips of adhesive plaster, small scissors, eye ointment, 3 in. wide elastic washable crepe bandage. Note that, for soft hands, it is a better idea to stick on a strip of plaster around the base of the thumb *before* the blister begins from long paddling. My hands rarely blister now but they feel quite soft. Probably because they are soaked with barrier cream from GRP canoe building. Sun-burn ointment and insect repellent will also be useful as will a tin of zinc ointment.

Repair kit

For GRP canoes I have a big roll of 1 in. sticky backed PVC tape, which basically is all one needs for day by day repairs. I carry a largish box of glass mat, a gallon of PA resin, catalyst, brush, cleaner, tubes of barrier and cleansing creams in the car. It would be impracticable to take all that afloat.

My repair kit is quite interesting being composed mainly of left-overs from canvas canoeing days. It has the large roll of sticky tape, a cigar tube containing oiled cotton wool and sailmakers needles, a block of beeswax, an 8 mm. film reel with tough thread wound onto it, a cobblers knife, and an old stainless steel razor blade. It continues to surprise me how often I use the kit, for stitching up my brief case, daughter's school bag, wind-torn tent, torn seat of wet suit and so on. It goes everywhere with me in canoes.

Waterproof bags

There are several kinds from which to choose. The best type are these composed of one bag inside another and sealed at the neck; the space between is inflated making a buoyancy bag as well as protecting the contents.

The cheapest way, and quite effective if done with care, is to use farmer's fertiliser bags, one inside the other. Polythene sheet from which the bags are made comes in various gauges, and I would never use less than 500 gauge. Most fertiliser bags are 1,000 gauge. Some bags are available in the form of proofed nylon outer bags, about 8 in. diameter and 3 ft. long, with neck ties, containing PVC inner bags the same shape. The inner bag should be just over half filled and the neck gathered up and tied and then turned over and tied again. This is then dropped into the outer bag, upside down, and the outer bag rolled over and tied as for the inner bag. I find that three bags will take everything that I carry for camping purposes.

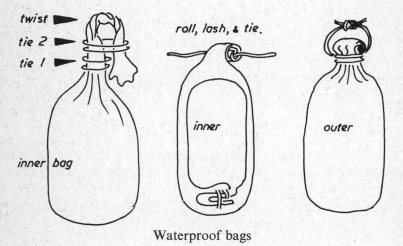

Waterproof bags

Few bags are completely successful in their purpose and at present some of the Guild of Canoe Builders and Designers are experimenting with an idea to seal off the whole of the back end of the canoe into which equipment may be loaded and kept fairly dry even in a swamping. The essence of the idea is to fit the hole in the back of the bucket seat with a rim to which an oval seal can be fixed by elastic cuff, like a cockpit rim and spray deck. The space between seat, hull and deck is sealed with expanding resin foam poured into place and cast *in situ*.

Securing bags to canoe

The bags should have ties at the neck to which other cords may be fastened. I push two long bags into the rear of the canoe, side by side, necks towards the cockpit. Securing cords tie to loops resined and glassed to the canoe sides or to holes drilled in the seat sides.

One bag goes into the bows in front of the footrest and ties to the holes drilled in the footrest brackets.

Dispersal of bags in canoe

The two bags behind the cockpit being close to the centre of the canoe should contain the heavy gear so as to reduce, as far as possible, the increase in rotational inertia which would take place if weight were placed at the far ends. One contains tent and cooking equipment and some food in cans. The other contains small items, more food, spare clothing, repair kit, first aid, etc.

The bow bag, being of necessity close to the end of the canoe in a restricted space, must be small and easily compressed into place; in order to put it in, it will be necessary to remove the buoyancy bag for which it must double. Therefore, one puts the sleeping bag up there maybe with the inflatable mattress also. In larger canoes one may keep the gear in the back of the canoe by using a partly inflated mattress as a bung behind the seat, trapping the gear behind it.

If the canoe is packed as suggested, even though all the heavy gear is at the back, provided it is close behind the cockpit it will be found that the balance of the canoe will be almost unchanged. The extra leverage of the light bow bag just about balances the small leverage of the heavy bags behind the cockpit.

If any equipment is to be kept in the cockpit area, it must be small, packed into its own small waterproof bag and wedged and tied behind the flanges at the sides of the seat. Open sided seats should have the gear fixed back to the canoe sides under the deck. There should never be any loose equipment or dangling lines in the cockpit area which may trap the body in a capsize.

Some of the small things, such as whistle, compass and flare pack should be kept in the anorak pocket.

SEA CANOEING

Sea canoeing makes very different demands on the canoe and its equipment. The necessity for rescue in deep water is very real, and the detailed items to be carried have differences.

For the Sea Proficiency Certificate test set by the British Canoe Union one requires the camping gear already mentioned. I don't propose to go through all that again. I shall describe what I take to sea with me and give reasons for its inclusion.

For sea canoeing one requires:

Emergency shelter; emergency food; emergency signals; reserve clothing; first aid equipment; extra paddle; extra lifejacket; extra buoyancy materials in the canoe; deck lines on the canoe.

Emergency shelter

The section on exposure shows that one may find it vital to place the patient out of the wind. A survival blanket, or a large 1,000 gauge plastic bag, 8 ft. by 4 ft. will be the minimum. A sleeping bag doubling as a buoyancy bag is very useful in addition. A tent would do very well especially one with a sewn-in ground sheet.

Emergency food

I carry a Horlicks Two-Man food pack and a four pint bottle of water. That should do for a week at a pinch. Hour by hour needs are satisfied by carrying chocolate and a can of fruit juice. Again, the requirements of treatment for exposure may indicate the need for either a small stove or a block of solid fuel and a 'Tommy Cooker'. It may be feasible to carry a flask of hot soup also or a self-heating can of Horlicks.

Emergency signals

One requires a whistle but that isn't much good when the going is really difficult. A torch comes next for convenience and signalling and then a pack of miniflares. I prefer the German 'Wischo' signal pen with explosive capsules. The explosive flare capsule does make a very noticeable bang high in the air and sound may be perceived more readily than light. These small flares are not much use for attracting attention but are used by the Royal National Lifeboat Institution for inshore signalling and pin-pointing a position. The Schermuly 'Mars' hand-held flare is very good for pinpointing a position when searchers have been alerted. It does not throw up flares roman candle fashion. The performance of some of the latter which I have seen has been either non-existent or so variable as to reduce confidence in them.

Notice that in each case so far the flare suggested is not much good for attracting attention. Smoke flares, unless they are very large and persistent, fade away too soon and wind disperses the smoke very rapidly. The 'Icarus' rocket flare by Schermuly is quite expensive but it sends up a parachute flare to a great height where it burns for many seconds. Details of performance may be obtained from most ships chandlers, yachtsmen's suppliers and so on. If every offshore seagoing canoeist carried one Icarus flare, three Mars hand flares and a Miniflare pack, no group would ever be short of signalling power.

One very simple visual signal, especially for the capsized canoeist in waves above two feet high, is to raise the paddle vertically in the air and hold it there. That really can be seen from a long way off, it is at once recognisable as a distress signal and it pinpoints the position. It is quite possible to be quite out of visual touch with the group, even though the furthest away is not more than fifty yards, when the intervening water is humped up into six feet waves cutting out visual contact.

Reserve clothing

The demands of treatment for exposure may be such as to require the patient to be re-clothed. A spare woollen sweater, windproof overtrousers and a windproof anorak should be the absolute minimum to be carried, with a woollen cap for the head, or better, a balaclava which will cover the face and neck to some extent. A dry towel stored in the same bag will also be useful for drying and for wrapping around the neck and head to retain warmth.

First aid equipment

Basically this should be the same as described on page 211 but if one is trapped on a rocky shore or offshore island there may be some danger of deep wounds and fractured limbs from a landing on rocks. I can only suggest that the canoeist carries two or three triangular bandages or a large reel of surgical strapping. Surgical strapping can pull the edges of gaping wounds together and may strap a broken leg to its partner for support or an arm to the side or chest. The difficulty would be in making adhesive plaster stick to wet salty skin. It may be that the canoe repair roll of tape will do instead of surgical tape.

Sticky tape for minimum first aid and repair kit.

Extra paddle

A jointed paddle, of the now rather old-fashioned type, which joins at a central ferrule would pack into a canoe cockpit behind the seat side flanges and would do if one of the group lost or broke his paddle.

Extra lifejacket

The reasons for this are obvious: it serves as extra buoyancy in the canoe when not used as a lifejacket and I could envisage a situation on a windy island where a lifejacket could blow off into the sea and away.

Extra buoyancy material

It is a good idea, when preparing a canoe for sea use, to make up a number of small and tough plastic bags stuffed with scraps of expanded polystyrene foam in order to make bags of large bulk with little weight. These are then wedged all around the gear already carried. The whole lot may be trapped in the back of the canoe by using an inflated air bag. The little bags are expendable and it doesn't matter much if one or two are lost out of a dozen or so.

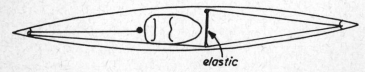

elastic

Deck lines

One method
of attaching
tow line

tow

Deck lines

Deck lines are essential on a sea going canoe. They are not essential for river canoes as end loops or strops are usually enough. On the sea, however, it is sometimes necessary to tow a weary paddler to safety. On the river one just goes ashore for a rest.

The deck lines should be rigged bow and stern, so that they are tight, and fixed through end loops to tying points at each side of the deck level with the front of the cockpit. The towing should be done from a point just behind the cockpit or by a line wrapped once around one's upper arm and held in the teeth for quick release. The principle is that, if towing is done from end to end, the two canoes pull into line and turning for the rescuer is very difficult. The towed canoe should be pulled by the bows and the towing canoe should offer the tow from the centre.

Tight deck lines are also useful when pulling or holding the canoe during a rescue in deep water.

Chapter 18

Exposure

The human animal requires a surrounding temperature of about 85 deg. F if it is not to feel cooled. A naked body in air at that degree of warmth will feel comfortable but it must be a naked *dry* body in *still* air.

Canoeists should wear clothes which are suitable for canoeing. 'Proper' clothing is partly a matter of personal preference and partly a matter of human need. If certain well-proved principles are borne in mind then the choice of clothing is narrowed considerably.

This section sets out to describe the principles involved and the currently accepted ways of achieving the desired ends.

Body distribution of heat

It is necessary to keep the heart, brain, lungs and other vital organs at a proper working temperature. Overheated, one becomes feverish. Overcooled, one becomes comatose and incapable of movement. It is possible to wear so many clothes that one has difficulty in becoming cool but the body heat as a result of exercise rises to uncomfortable levels. What is required is the absolute minimum of clothing which will allow canoeing to go on in relative comfort.

Let us consider the body as having a core and a surface. The core contains the vital organs and the surface, the skin and limbs. It is possible to cool the surface to very low temperatures so that frostbite may result. This is not necessarily a fatal condition but if prolonged one may lose toes, fingers and ear lobes because the cessation of blood flow to the affected parts has allowed necrosis of the tissue to begin. This does not necessarily happen only in extreme cold. One man suffered in the Devizes to Westminster race mainly because the enormous demands on the muscles in racing canoeing over a long time took so much blood from his surface tissues on a cold night that his skin 'died' in patches on his face and hands. He required treatment for nearly a year as a result. Others travelling less quickly with less effort were not affected.

The body loses heat mostly from places usually exposed to cold air. These places are the face, head, neck, chest and the lining of the lungs and throat. Doing heavy physical work, depth and rate of breathing are increased and considerable volumes of cold air are sucked right into one of the vital organs there to be warmed up to body heat and blown out at once. A lot of body heat is lost almost at the heart of the matter.

The face is usually exposed so that perception of one's surroundings is enhanced. This causes the face to feel cold when the wind blasts the tops of the waves right into it. The salt irritates the eyes and pain in the facial sinuses is often experienced. A nagging headache is often associated with an upset stomach and sickness reduces the ability of the body to produce the necessary effort to go on paddling in what may be difficult conditions. Keep your face warm. Cover your ears. This means that one loses sensitivity to one's surroundings which may or may not matter. The choice may be made on the spot but be prepared.

Covering the neck, the top of the head and the chest and upper arms is not difficult and should not interfere with the action of canoeing.

Generation of body heat

The body operates at about 98.4 deg. F, 37 deg. C. It can go down to about 90 deg. F without fatal results and people who are trained to swim in very cold conditions will manage to continue to exist quite happily in conditions which would stop lesser mortals. Body heat is generated by the breakdown of food in the system into energy which the muscles can use. It is necessary to have food in the body for it to feel warm. If you want advice on how your body will best generate heat, consult your doctor.

The mind has a considerable effect on the workings of the body. A determination to do well may not be the only requirement but it does help. The mind acts in mysterious ways. One's state of mind at the time is not what wins or loses the day, so much as what one has been for years; the sort of person one is, the way one makes decisions, the tenacity with which one persists in what is being done. The big strong man may not necessarily do better than the little fellow. In other words, survival is not just of the body it is a matter of education and the way in which one usually employs body and mind; it is spirit. The spirit cannot be commanded to do this or that in emergencies. It simply is what it is. It may change as the result of the emergency but that is in the future and is a result and not a cause.

The state of mind affects the temperature of the body. The nervous system is linked to blood vessels and these, especially surface blood vessels, can be dilated to increase the blood flow through them or constricted to reduce it. This is not a conscious act. Emotional states of mind affect the autonomic nervous system; one feels embarrassed and the blood flow is increased to the face. Whilst normally, in cold conditions, the autonomic nervous system will restrict blood flow to the skin and with it, of course, the body warmth carried by the blood, in extreme states of shock as a result of continued extreme cold, the nervous system may lose its grip and allow the blood flow to run unrestricted to the surface thus permitting a catastrophic and fatal loss of heat at the core.

Fear, apprehension, doubt; all these emotions can affect the state of the blood flow in the body causing temporary variations from normal. Loss of heat from the body is controlled not only by insulating clothing or by the intake of food—the degree of emotional stability is a relevant factor.

Loss of body heat

Heat is transferred from one place to another by several different methods. In the case of the sun high energy radiation is what gives life to us all.

The body temperature is at a low level compared with fire. The temperature difference between skin at, say, 45 deg. F and water at 38 deg. F is very small. Radiation of heat from the body is insignificant. If the body is placed in water some heat will be lost through conduction. The warmed water will rise away and take with it the body warmth and fresh cold water will take its place;

convection currents are established and heat is lost continually. If, however, one traps the warmed water in contact with the skin it will provide a warm barrier between the body and further heat loss as a result of contact with cold water.

By far the most serious source of heat loss comes when a wet body is exposed to a blowing wind. The water on the body evaporates and takes with it vast quantities of heat from the body. After a serious accident on the Peak District hills some years ago, experiments were conducted to find at what temperatures the body could keep on working. A subject operated a bicycle device and his work rate, pulse, respiration rates, etc., were all measured. Apparently when naked and dry in still air, he worked quite well. When wet all over, but in still air, he worked well, with little heat loss. But when wet and with air blowing over him at six m.p.h. he suffered a heat loss which would have been fatal in a short time if it had continued. The answer to this is to keep moving air from the wet body when it is out of the water. In the water, of course, the air cannot blow over the body. That is why some will say that it is warmer in the water than out when it is breezy, even though the water temperature is lower than the air temperature.

Clothing to prevent loss of body heat

It is clear that suitable clothing can reduce heat loss to a tolerable minimum. Dr Pugh in his article *Accidental Hypothermia in Campers, Climbers and Walkers* which appeared in the *British Medical Journal* for 16th January 1966, considered the cases of many people caught on the hills, who died or needed treatment for exposure. In almost every case they were wet and exhausted.

One begins canoeing by getting wet. Some people can enjoy canoeing and remain triumphantly dry. Some have been known to say 'I don't intend to get wet', and really they believe it. My kind of canoeing soon disposes of fancy notions like that. Let us assume that one will become wet when canoeing and that it will happen at the least opportune moment when the going is really hard. This is very often when one is tired or even exhausted. Remember, then, that physical weariness must be allowed for during an emergency. Physical weariness is partly the result of continuous loss of energy and heat is energy; conserve heat and one's 'range' is extended. One is less weary if warm. Wetness does

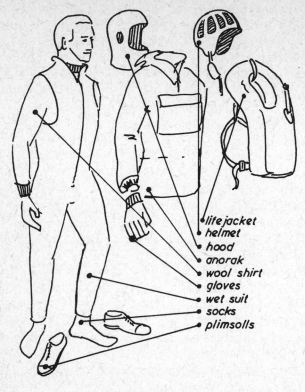

life jacket
helmet
hood
anorak
wool shirt
gloves
wet suit
socks
plimsolls

Protective clothing

not matter if one is warm.

Free movement of the arms is essential. Close one hand over the other forearm and open and close the fingers of the arm which is held. You will feel considerable muscular movement from the finger movements. This movement is all in the forearm. Good paddling demands that the fingers should be continuously opening and closing; restrict this movement and the waste products of muscular movement build up in the muscles and pain results. This is because the blood cannot flow so readily through constricted blood vessels. If one is suffering from pain concentration is weakened. If one loses concentration in difficult circumstances one may lose balance and be plunged into the water with possibly fatal results. Physical strength is impaired by the restricted blood flow in the forearms and most rescue techniques require strength in the fingers for gripping cords and canoes.

Close-fitting sleeves restrict arm movements and cause chafing at the armpits. Soreness, especially of the tender skin under the arms, causes pain which reduces concentration, etc. From the shoulders to the wrists there should be easy movement.

The body should be clothed warmly in a lined wet-suit and closely woven woollen shirt. The closest that the nervous system comes to the surface is in its journey through the spinal cord. Stun the nerves with cold, and they function erratically, if at all. So an extra thickness of insulation along the length of the spine from hindquarters to head would seem to be a good thing. Muscular movements of the trunk are less extensive and so close fitting materials can, and must, be used. This close fitting is necessary to limit free movement of trapped water which if free to move would carry away body heat.

The legs are not used except in static balance, and in a well equipped canoe the spray deck will contain heat from the lower limbs. However, although close fitting leg protection is not necessary when one is in the canoe, it is when one is in the water that the heat insulation is essential. The legs should be enclosed in a close fitting wet-suit.

Wet-suit material, usually neoprene with a nylon lining, is, to some extent, porous and will soak up water which it releases later in evaporation. It is therefore rather chilling to wear a soaked wet suit in a cold wind. This is the usual state of affairs when one is in the canoe and it is, therefore, necessary to enclose the close-fitting wet-suit in an airproof top. The anorak, made of lightweight proofed nylon fabric, is best for this. A long kagul is an embarrassment in the canoe, being too long. Proofed over-trousers may also be worn for complete protection but this is gilding the lily a little. It may be a good idea to carry them in the canoe on an extended offshore trip during which a temporary landing is expected.

The feet should be protected with thick woollen socks and plimsolls or, better still, neoprene wet-suit socks over which are fitted firmly laced and larger than usual plimsolls. As a matter of interest, a canoeist's plimsolls can always be recognised because they are worn thin, or through, on the outer part of each heel where the tilted foot rubs the floor of the canoe. The main function of the plimsoll is to ease walking over rough ground when carrying a canoe on the shoulder and to prevent cut feet when landing on rocks or litter strewn beaches. Plimsolls must be firmly laced otherwise the fast moving water in a capsize and wipe-out plucks them off the feet.

The head is a major site of heat loss. The neoprene helmet which goes with a wet-suit is useful, but restricting. Ear holes must be cut so that hearing is possible. Conditions are difficult enough at sea without muffling the hearing. The hood should come well down over the forehead to restrict heat loss; the neck should be covered but not tightly. It is extraordinary how difficult it is to find a reason for one's splitting headache when wearing a really good warm but tight collar. On top of all this it is more frequent these days to find canoeists wearing plastic crash helmets. These are very necessary in deep water rescues when entry between the canoes may be accompanied by an inward swing of the canoes alongside just as the head is in line with the hard gunwales. Launching from breakwaters and promenades into a bumpy sea and looping in surf requires a helmet. One drawback in Force 6 winds is a thrumming roar through the slots, which these helmets must have to spill water when rolling. The roar effectively blots out all aural communication. In addition to the helmet there may be a face mask. Apparently the face mask, such as ice hockey goal minders wear, has been tried by some sea canoeists. Such a mask would reduce pain from chilled facial sinuses and from stinging slashing wind borne spray . . . but an itchy nose would be a difficult thing to deal with, I suppose.

Finally, hands are sensitive and can be painful if not protected. A pair of cheap household plastic gloves with knitted cuffs are the very thing and keep the hands tolerably warm. Neoprene mitts are useless as they slip about on the paddle shaft.

STAGES OF HYPOTHERMIA

Dr Pugh's article, previously referred to, gives a very clear idea of how severe cooling of the body will affect a walker. One of the first stages is that control of the legs is lost. Walkers totter about, stagger, stand quite still or fall down. As a canoeist is already sitting down these stages may go unnoticed by the canoeist until

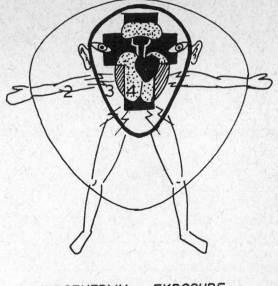

HYPOTHERMIA — EXPOSURE.

STAGES   1. EXTREMITIES.
          2. LIMBS, HEARING.
          3. COMA, CO-ORDINATION.
          4. CEREBELLUM, HEART.

he tries to get out of his canoe. However, his hands will be cold, his grip shaky and his paddling action slow. He will complain of numbness in the legs, perhaps sickness as a result of an empty stomach and natural apprehension. This may be the same thing as the 'kayak fear' of the Greenland seal hunters.

At this stage the mind is suffering a sensation of general discomfort and apprehension. If this is recognised then one should at once set about changing the conditions which give rise to it. Find shelter, eat some chocolate or have a hot drink. Do not take alcohol, however, because its effects are too unpredictable. It may give a feeling of euphoria, but it reduces the control the body has over the skin temperature and this may result in a serious loss of body heat.

After a short time the paddler may act irrationally, exhibit a sudden burst of energy, refuse to talk or gabble incessantly, not

L.C.8

answer questions. The result is rather like drunkenness. The brain is being cooled and is losing its power to think and act. Hearing is muffled and sight affected in that one sees double or focuses slowly. Colour balance is affected—the sky looks dark green, the sun bright blue. Different people may be affected in different ways but the general symptoms will be of much the same order.

If swimming in the water, a general feeling of numbness not of cold may occur. One has a reluctance to time the breathing to coincide with the surge of wave tops over the head, a feeling of 'Why bother?' Soon after this consciousness fades, returns, fades and then fails to return. There is sudden collapse. The patient lapses into coma and recovery is doubtful. Death may follow in seconds perhaps preceded by convulsions.

What has happened is that steady cooling has steadily lowered the body core temperature despite the body's defences. Sluggishness of limb movements reflects the cooling of the muscles, numbness is the result of the cessation of blood flow to the surface tissues and to the deeper muscles in the extremities. As the cooling continues the brain is no longer able to operate properly. When the conscious grip on oneself is lost, the autonomic nervous system is alone maintaining life. This can fail quite suddenly if the surface warms up and the core receives a fatal charge of cold blood from the surface as the blood vessels on the surface dilate.

Treatment in the absence of a doctor

Your first duty to the patient is to send for a doctor. However, it is in the nature of things that canoeing takes place in remote places where communication is difficult. Flares may attract the attention of helicopters or watchful coastguards. There are hundreds of miles of coast in the far North West where watchers are few and distress signals may not be seen. What to do then? In any event, it may be a long time before a doctor can come to the patient.

1. Remove patient from the cooling influence. Prevent further cooling.
2. Carry him with his head below the level of his feet in order to improve blood supply to the brain.
3. Take him to a warm building or shelter from the wind.
4. Cover him with windproof clothing, a sleeping bag or tent.

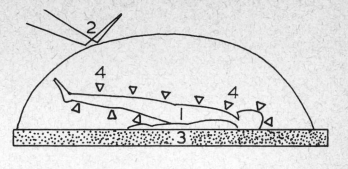

1. *Patient head low.*

2. *Keep wind off.*

3. *Insulate from ground.*

4. *Supply heat.*

Hypothermia—treatment

5. Put him in a hot bath; as hot as the elbow can stand. Temperature 112 deg. F. This temperature is quite critical.

6. Strip him in the bath. If breathing ceases use mouth to mouth resuscitation, and don't stop until breathing begins again or a doctor says he's dead. Keep him in the bath during this. Keep the water temperature up with charges of hot water but don't scald the patient.

7. When patient begins to sweat, take him out, dry him and put him to bed.

8. After a couple of hours of sleep he will probably feel fine and on top of the world. Keep him quiet even then. Next day he will probably be quite well but slow.

9. If there is no bath or shelter, then put him in a sleeping bag.

10. Ask someone else, who is warm and fit, to climb in the bag with him.

11. Put them into a tent to keep off the wind. If there is no tent a large plastic bag will do.

12. Prepare hot soup, or hot cocoa. Keep his head low except when feeding hot drinks.

13. Keep him off the ground even if it means lying under him.

L.C.9

14. He will warm up more quickly in the bag if both patient and rescuer are stripped.
15. As with mouth to mouth resuscitation a certain 'prudery' must be overcome if one is to put the maintenance of life first.

Chapter 19

An Instructor's Responsibilities

Certain key words have proved useful to me when arranging teaching sequences. These words are

FUN   SAFETY   DISCIPLINE   CHALLENGE

Fun is fear overcome, self-explored, boundaries of experience set further back. It is not necessarily the banana skin joke although canoeing provides many such situations.

Safety began when the person in charge learned to swim. It was increased when the pupil learned to swim. The lifejacket added its quota of safety, and so on. Safety is not an absolute condition. Please don't ever say to an anxious parent 'Mary, or Bill, will be perfectly safe whilst canoeing'. They won't you know. Step within five feet of a puddle of water two inches deep and there is a small risk of drowning. However, life is bound to end with a fatal experience. It is just a matter of where, when and how. Safety is an attitude of mind. Be practical and don't try to allay natural anxieties with empty promises. It is better that Mary or Bill should not go afloat at all than that you should make false promises. Don't deceive yourself.

Discipline has its roots in the word disciple—those who followed in order to learn. If it is necessary to command someone to do something against the will the result is unlikely to be successful but if the person willingly follows a difficult series of exercises in order to learn, then success is almost certain. If the introduction to canoeing is fun, then discipline is likely to be welcome.

Challenge is the natural state of the human animal. Most people welcome a challenge. Challenges may be person to person, person against time, or distance, or self or nature. It may be a combination of all or any of these. The simple act of the first capsize is to some possibly the biggest challenge that they will experience in canoeing.

Lest it seem that there has been an undue dwelling upon the lethal nature of canoeing, one should put it in relation to the lethal nature of almost any other human activity. It is a matter of taking care. A good maxim is to ask oneself, before beginning a session in charge of other people, 'What would I say to the Coroner?' This should ensure a mental review of all the factors for and against safety for the group.

Basic attitudes to one's charges are very much a matter of the personality. Whatever is suggested as a proper mode of progress will be interpreted in terms of one's own experience and prejudice. However, there can be little argument that one owes to one's charges certain responsibilities. These are that one must be able to ensure, as far as one is able, that they receive.

AIR, WARMTH, DRINK, FOOD, in that order.

A supply of air is ensured by keeping the pupil's nose and mouth above water at all times whatever the conditions. The first capsize makes nonsense of that. So now a certain education is necessary in order to cause people to remember to hold their breath and blow water out of the nose when submerged. Education, swimming ability, experience in swimming baths and a proper lifejacket should provide for all but a very small number of occasions.

Warmth is most important. If sufficient body warmth is lost the power of voluntary movement is lost, thinking is chaotic, involuntary muscle movement (heart and lungs) ceases and death ensues. It is up to you to see that the group is properly clothed and fed.

Drink is of more urgent necessity than food to the human animal. Drink can be cold or hot, bland or intoxicating, stimulant or sedative. Hot soup takes a bit of whacking after a day in the surf. Alcoholic drink may have the opposite effect to that desired.

Food is a matter which affects the canoeist both before and after the event. A good breakfast before a long day at sea or down a river is a good thing, because lunch will almost certainly be a matter of sandwiches. Chocolate bars, being waterproof, are a good thing to have about the boat or one's person. This is a matter for the good sense of the members of the group.

It is the Instructor's responsibility to inform himself about the water that the group is to use, about the members of the group and so on.

To whom does one go for advice? To those who have experienced the problems themselves and who can give forewarning. When going to a strange coast chat with the coastguards about tide races and tidal flows. In other words, consult those who know.

It pays you to obtain information from the people who have experience of canoeing in every part of the British Isles and in most parts of the world. These people are mostly members of the British Canoe Union in this country, or of the Scottish Canoe Association in Scotland. The British Canoe Union has a Coaching Scheme and much of what follows has been learned by watching and talking with other members of the BCU and the SCA, the Army Canoeing Union and so on.

If you have the British Canoe Union's Senior Instructors Certificate you have at least prepared yourself as fully as one might reasonably expect you to do. You are in a position to draw upon considerable technical resources and advice from many experienced canoeists who have already made all the mistakes you are likely to make.

That is a fair 'puff' for the Union. You know, of course, that it is the collective strength of an organised group that wins friends and influences people. The right of access to your bit of water that you have used for years may be forfeit unless some organised body defends your right to use it. The Ribble is a case at present in issue, as canoeing is almost at a standstill on it, and the local authorities, fishing interests, Sports Advisory Council, and the BCU are all considering what should be done.

The BCU Coaching Scheme is, very briefly, as follows: There are Proficiency Certificates, and Coaching Awards.

Novice Canoeing Test: For youngsters at school.

Inland Proficiency Certificate, Kayak. Basic test for all, double ended paddle.

Inland Proficiency Certificate, Canadian. Single bladed paddle.

Sea and Open Water Proficiency Certificate, Kayak only.

A bronze badge is awarded for any or all of these attainments. There is a small fee for each examination.

Advanced Inland Kayak Certificate. Usually requires two years at the game.

Advanced Inland Canadian Certificate. (There are two quite

different types of Canadian paddling now, traditional and European slalom. The certificate may be given for either, but future practice will probably require competence in both.)

Advanced Sea Test. This is as much chart work as sea work. A silver badge is awarded for competence in one or two of these, but for all three the Gold Award is obtained.

The Coaching Awards are:

Assistant Instructor. This is a minimum qualification.

Senior Instructor. This is what most teachers should aim for. One may examine for the proficiency awards but only those which one has passed oneself.

Coach. This person has two Advanced Certificates, has a wide experience of canoeing at a competitive level, is competent in most forms of canoe, can ride a K1, or thrash through a Grade 3 rapid. He has probably two years at least of first class experience, including organisation of events.

Senior Coach. Has, or should have, a Gold Award for Proficiency, has probably served as an Area Coaching Organiser, or is so serving, his life is centred on canoeing, he writes about his experiences, passes on ideas and tries always to improve canoeing experience. All the present Senior Coaches have at least eight years experience. This is an appointment, not an award.

The British Canoe Union Coaching Scheme has been reconsidering the standards and names of the standards given here. The new standards (at the time of revision) have not yet been decided, but new standards there will be. For up-to-date information, please write to the British Canoe Union, Coaching Scheme, 70 Brompton Road, London SW3 1DT.

Chapter 20

Organising a Baths Training Course

Without doubt, the best way in which to begin canoeing is in the swimming baths. Natural hazards are reduced to a minimum and the group may concentrate on learning paddling skills. The water is contained within a small area, easy to scan at a glance, it is warm and it does not rush by carrying off canoes, gear and bodies. One may see what is happening both above water and below water. Wind roar and the chilly blasts of summer do not make instruction impossible. One may prepare in winter for summer.

The following ideas have developed with the types of canoe in use and follow a natural sequence. This begins to take shape when the novice is asked 'What is it that worries you most about canoeing?' Usually the answer will be, 'What do I do when it turns over?' It is desirable that the canoeist should be a swimmer before instruction begins; however, I would be quite happy to allow a non-swimmer, who is keen to try out a canoe in a swimming bath under my undivided attention, to do so if only to give him or her a good reason for learning to swim. A total ban on non-swimmers in canoes is too severe.

In a swimming bath, but always with the safety of each member in mind, I would take more people under my control than on outside waters, but not more than sixteen if I were unaided. Much depends on the composition of the group—with a really good assistant instructor twenty may be the maximum.

It is essential to test whether the class are swimmers; question and answer is not enough. Therefore, the first part of every session is a one hundred yard swim. The fast swimmers will do it in half the time that the ordinary swimmer will, but all must try. For every 25 yd. of swim there should be two obstacles, canoes across the line of swim perhaps, steadied by assistants or other non-

233

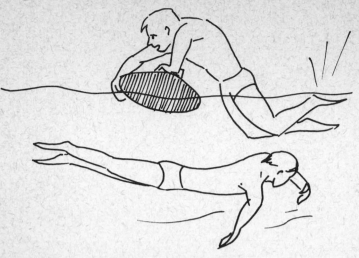

'Over and under' drill

participants. The swimmer comes to a canoe and alternately swims over or under them. This is quite exhausting and results in bruised fingers, thick ears, scratches and severe loss of breath. Good! The first steps towards experiencing the problems of deep water rescue techniques have been taken. The swimming becomes incidental to a big challenge which, in itself, is a discipline and a safety factor and becomes great fun as the crashing and splashing continues. This drill is also a very good fitness developer; I call it 'Over and Under'. Every session begins with it and ends with at least a 50 yd. unencumbered swim.

Launch the canoes. No need to make a big thing of this, as one had to with canvas canoes which were likely to leave their coaming frames in one's hands; GRP canoes will take a great deal of hard treatment that would damage lesser canoes. Again, it may be argued that one should demonstrate the proper way to enter a canoe (see page 240). Of course they will capsize, but who cares in these conditions? I prefer it, in fact. However, an important safety factor is to have each canoe in the hands of two people, one working and one watching and helping.

The pupil climbs into the canoe and sets off to paddle around the baths, collisions and all, using hands only. Some will capsize or have difficulty in making the canoe do what is required, but

within five minutes almost everyone will be thrashing about the bath, arms whirling, soaking wet and, very likely, happy. This is a good frame of mind in which to learn. It is remarkable how easily and naturally the untutored hand paddler moves the canoe using quite sophisticated techniques with the hands. The move back to square one begins when the paddle is put into his hands.
Bring the class to order, arrange a change of place between the pupil and his assistant, and then repeat the whole thing. Ensure that the class has bath towels or old sweaters to keep their shoulders covered whilst they take their turn to watch.

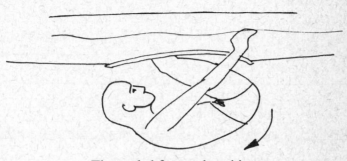

The curled forward position

Now one arranges the first demonstration. The teacher, or his assistant, climbs into a canoe, hand paddles to the centre of the baths and demonstrates the curled forward position. He capsizes, thumps the bottom of the canoe, rolls out and swims to the shallow end using the back stroke and pulling the canoe.
The second demonstration follows at once, showing how to empty the canoe single-handed (see page 242). Certain principles may be discussed here. The demonstration of putting one's head up into the upturned cockpit to breath the air entrapped there is a good idea as it ensures that the pupil can be shown a good reason for *not* attempting to turn his canoe the right way up after a capsize. It is a good idea to demonstrate also what happens if one panics and attempts to climb up onto the canoe from the side; it rolls over and over, spilling air, taking in water and sinking.
The class then goes afloat, two to each canoe, one in the canoe and one watching and the capsize drill is done under direction.

The first capsize is done under close attention. It is usually clearly to be seen at this stage who are the doubtful paddlers and who have confidence. The doubtful ones may go so far as to ask if capsizing is really necessary. I reply by asking them if, having thought about it, they really do wish to canoe? They usually answer yes, seeing that they are in the class in the first place. I then ask if they wish to receive my instruction. They have answered yes (up to now, that is). Therefore, I say, they must tackle this job in my way. Obviously it is the capsize which worries them, otherwise they would not be jibbing at it, so I suggest they do it or forever put canoeing aside. Always practise the move which gives the most difficulty.

The capsize drills done, I usually relax the discipline and allow the canoeists to paddle around freely using paddles for the first time. This is for me a state of *apparent* inactivity. I am watching with great keenness the people who seemed doubtful about capsizing, and I also ensure that each watcher is watching. I am not in the water myself. If the session is the usual 45 minute affair, the work done so far will have taken up all the available time. One may finish off with a short rolling demonstration, followed invariably by the 50 yards swim.

The first session will have produced a crop of questions. The very best way in which to give instruction is to have the pupil asking questions arising naturally out of the experience.

The next session may follow immediately, but I would prefer, on a one-day course, to have a coffee break at the stage when people begin to ask questions and answer them during this break.

Begin the next session with one hundred yards swim, over and under. Everyone in turn then climbs into a canoe and practises capsize drill under the watchful eye of the partner and under your general care. The air should resound to the thumps of hands on upturned canoes. Try to introduce an air of urgency into the proceedings. Urgency without haste is the watchword in GRP canoe building and in deep water rescues. It is a good frame of mind to inculcate. Remind each that his partner is waiting for his turn.

Following this practice, demonstrate entering the canoe, adjusting the spray deck, holding the paddles and paddling about generally. Move the canoe to the centre of the baths and talk about the sphere of movement. Demonstrate paddling forwards, stopping, paddling backwards, stopping, with increasing energy. Indicate that this is a useful warming up exercise on first going afloat. If one can make a thing move it must be in the sure knowledge that one can stop it at will.

Having demonstrated the first straight line movement, go on to the first turning movement—the sweep turn. Ask the class how the canoe can be turned. The first answer is, almost invariably, paddle on one side. So do that taking care that the paddle shaft is as close to the vertical as can be. Turning a slalom canoe through 360 deg. in the width of the pool in 12 or 16 strokes requires practice. Count the strokes aloud and ask, how may the rate of turn be improved. Usually one receives the answer, paddle backwards on the other side. So I alternately paddle forward on one side and then backward on the other, counting strokes and taking great care to keep the paddle upright. I usually turn the slalom canoe in 10 or 12 strokes. Not much improvement obviously. The class by now is deep in thought. How may the rate of turn be improved? Very few give the right answer, which relates to the angle of the paddle shaft. The shaft should be as close to the vertical as possible for a straight driving stroke and as close to the horizontal for a turning stroke. Putting the paddle as close to the horizontal as possible means placing the blade out wide. With a blade placed far out from the canoe side my turn is made in about four strokes. This may be reduced to two strokes if one lies well over to the outside of the turn and takes time between strokes.

The class now climbs in and practises capsize drill with spray deck, paddling forwards and backwards, stopping and turning. Let them have a free-for-all but ensure that generally they are practising the skills demonstrated. Ensure that each paddler has a watcher, of course.

Allow time at the end of the second session for a further demonstration. This is of rescue techniques and it is useful to take these in the order shown in Chapter 14. The swimmer to canoeist rescue is a good one for saving time during practice of further canoeing skills. If the paddler can rely on being hoisted upright by his assistant then time is saved in emptying the canoe out after a capsize and exit. Demonstrate the RLSS rescue technique for

L.C.9

swimmer to swimmer (I usually use the unigrip method) and have the class practise in pairs. Finish off the session with a two, three or four length swim. Hard work is good for the soul!

The third session begins with the over and under swim of one hundred yards, and goes on to a free practice of all previous drills; remind the class what these were before relinquishing close control. After ten or fifteen minutes demonstrate the second straight line movement, that is directly sideways using the draw stroke and the sculling draw stroke. Show the development of the draw stroke into the advanced support on a vertical shaft—most important. Always try to show the class what each of the basic drills can lead to and you will find the adventurous and gifted doing it without further instruction or practice.

From the second straight line movement go to the second turning movement, which is over. Demonstrate the slap support and the sculling support. I always explain that when I test people for their proficiency certificate I require them to do a good slap support with paddle in the normal grip so that the cockpit rim just touches the water. This must be repeated three times accurately. For advanced work I show them the slap support taken right over so that the head is immersed in the water and the recovery is almost a half roll. The sculling support requires a steady tilt on the canoe (not wobbling frantically on-off balance) so that the cockpit rim is touching the water for a steady count of ten. This soon shows which side the paddler is good on, which he usually practises and which side requires attention. Also, I show them the advanced development of the sculling support so that, Cheshire-cat-like, all that remains on the surface is a grin. It is remarkable how easy it is to lie deep in the water, with the sculling paddle gently wafting to and fro allowing one to support the head on the surface to take breath. The upward lunge is achieved with the hip flick as used in rolling.

This is the end of the basic paddle strokes required for four of the six basic methods in the sphere of movement (see page 242). One explains that the up and down movement is produced by the waves, as is the looping movement. A good stunt is to illustrate these two wave-produced moves by having someone sit in a largish canoe whilst two others work the ends up and down like pump handles. A heavy storm may soon be developed in the baths and to ride a BAT in these conditions gives some idea of nasty short choppy waves. The looping may be shown by sitting in the BAT on the high dive board, say five feet from the water which must be at least 7 ft. deep, paddles in hand, and diving the whole lot off the top. Lean well back, and as the thing pops up one usually comes over sideways, requiring a roll up. Heavyweights have time to think, lightweights are spat back as with a stick thrown end-on into the water.

I should point out that these stunts with baths canoes are quite new, and a small, but select, band of canoeists of high technical ability never canoe outside the baths. Before tackling the stunts it is wise to have instruction in the methods to be used and the possible dangers.

Of course, not everyone believes in the value of stunts but I am convinced that the ability to handle the canoe and paddles, no matter in what novel attitude the canoe-body-paddle unit finds itself, is a good thing. Any stunt, the more comical the better provided danger of damage to canoe and paddler is remote, is well worth while.

The third session is rounded off with life-saving towing practice and a hundred yard swim. The exercise will keep one fit.

The fourth session is a rehash of all that has gone before, mostly free practice but the instructor should keep the latter half for demonstration and practice of new rescue techniques. The next to be shown should be the eskimo rescues, bow presentation and paddle presentation.

The fifth session should include a general talk on rolling drills, and these should be practised: assisted roll, hip flick practice, paddle drills dry and wet. Leave the actual rolling tuition to the fifth or sixth sessions. Maintain 'over and under' and life-saving towing drills at start and finish of each session as standard practice.

DEMONSTRATION PROCEDURES

Entering a canoe

1. Check that footrest position is suitable for your legs and put canoe in water alongside bath.
2. Wear spray deck, ensure that the release strap is fitted and that spray deck fits canoe.
3. Hitch back of spray deck above buttocks.

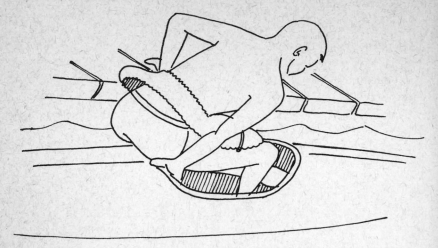

Entering a canoe

4. Kneel down on bath side facing the way that the canoe is pointing. Remember that the seat is toward the back of the cockpit.
5. Reach down with the canoe side hand and hold the front of the cockpit.
6. Place the bath side hand firmly on the bath side and *do not move it*.
7. Place the canoe side foot in the canoe, central and as far forward as the cockpit hole will permit.
8. Transfer canoe side hand to rear centre of cockpit. Do not move other hand.
9. Place other foot directly behind the first foot to enter the canoe.
10. Sit down, sliding one or both legs forward into front end of canoe taking weight on rear hand. This also ensures that the back of the spray deck remains tucked up around the waist.
11. Sit down into canoe and place hands on both sides of the cockpit, lift body and adjust position by wriggling back into seat. Capsize results if off-centre push is used.
12. Adjust spray deck, rear first, front next, sides last. Release strap *must* be outside ready for instant use.

Capsize drill

This is described in the section on rolling techniques. Having capsized, one goes to one or other end of the canoe (the upstream end in a fast moving stream) and swims, using a backstroke, to the shallow water. This enables the canoe to be emptied by one person without help. Note that if a GRP canoe has no additional buoyancy in it it will sink when all the air has spilled out because its specific gravity (1.3 to 1.6) is greater than that of water.

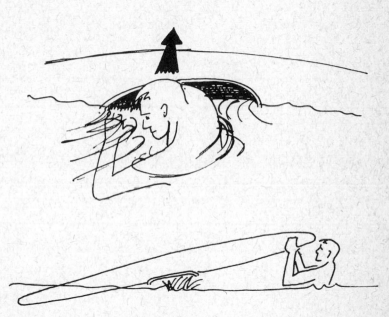

Capsize drill

Emptying canoe

1. Go to centre of canoe.
2. Turn cockpit towards you.
3. Place arm and shoulder inside cockpit.
4. Lift by thrusting steadily upwards with shoulder; balance with arm.

5. This should remove most of the 6-8 cwts of trapped water in half a minute.
6. With the cockpit uppermost go to the end of the canoe which normally lies highest above the water. This is almost always the front.
7. Press down so that top of deck lies on level of water.
8. Place other hand under the bows about six inches from the front.
9. Rotate the canoe towards you, keeping the bows down, until it is completely inverted with cockpit rim levelled off underneath.
10. Lift and the water which was trapped in the lower end nearest the canoeist will decant through the cockpit hole. Repeat three times from 6 above. Common fault is to allow the canoe to rock during the lift allowing water to flow past the cockpit side inside the canoe.

The sphere of movement

Laban's theories of movement relate to the cube of movement. I believe that this shape is too limiting and prefer the sphere which allows an infinite number of attitudes to be adopted. One should be competent to deal with any attitude or movement within the sphere.

The sphere has three axes which allow rotations in three planes. The canoe will move along or around these axes. The axes are the longitudinal, the lateral and the vertical. Movement along the longitudinal axis is movement straight forwards or backwards. Movement along the lateral axis is movement directly sideways. Movement along the vertical axis is wave produced and is up and down motion. Turning about the vertical axis is turning from left to right or vice versa. Turning about the longitudinal axis is turning over, either down left or down right ending in the complete roll. Turning about the transverse axis results in looping, end over end, either bow over stern or stern over bows. The loop is wave produced.

Diagonal movement in a straight line is a product of the move along the longitudinal axis and the move along the transverse axis. In surfing one may find the canoe sliding diagonally sideways, lifting to the following wave, and looping and rolling, all at the

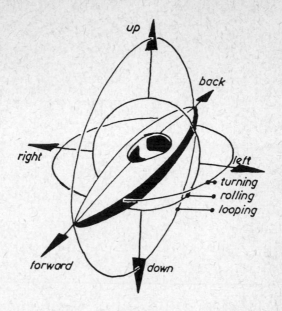

SPHERE OF MOVEMENT

same time. One learns to cope with that sort of confusing movement if the essentials are remembered which are the sphere and
its three axes of direction or rotation.

Re-entry from knee deep water

The BCU proficiency certificate once required that the candidate
should re-enter the canoe from knee deep water. This is often
difficult to arrange in a swimming bath unless the water is
unusually low. One way is to place a metal, or non-floating, chair
in the shallow end and stand on that before attempting to re-enter.

1. Stand alongside the cockpit in knee deep water.
2. Place the paddle in the canoe-side hand.
3. Place this hand at the rear off-side of the cockpit.
4. Place the thumb under the cockpit rim and fingers over the
   shaft of the paddle.
5. Put the canoe-side leg into cockpit.

Re-entry from knee-deep water

6. Place the behind over cockpit rim. This will require a transfer of balance from the foot on the bottom to the canoe. Drop down on to seat.
7. Place other hand on rear of cockpit opposite to the first hand.
8. Adjust position in canoe, using both hands for balance, leg trailing.
9. Lift other leg into canoe and adjust position again.

Wiggle/wriggle

Canoeing in baths may seem to some rather unenterprising and dull; all capsize drill and pottering about. Many challenge situations exist and can be used by beginners. One, which has a startling effect on the skill of beginners, is the wiggle test. It pressurises them in space and time and exhibits their deficiencies for everyone to see, especially themselves.

The gate is a horizontal strut rigged to hang about six feet above the water. Two vertical poles are suspended from it so that their inner edges are exactly four feet apart. The hanging poles are painted black and white in alternate 6 in. bands, white band just

above the surface. The cords which suspend the 54 in. long
vertical poles are adjusted so that the lower ends of the poles are
about 1 to 2 in. above the water surface.

The wiggle test requires the paddler to follow a set sequence of
moves, always the same, always on still water, always with the
same gate dimensions, in whatever part of the world he may be.
Bill Horseman who suggested the scheme as an International
competition envisaged trophies being awarded for this competition,
and this may yet take place. I find it of the greatest use in coaching
work. The moves are timed as the canoeist's bows enter the gate

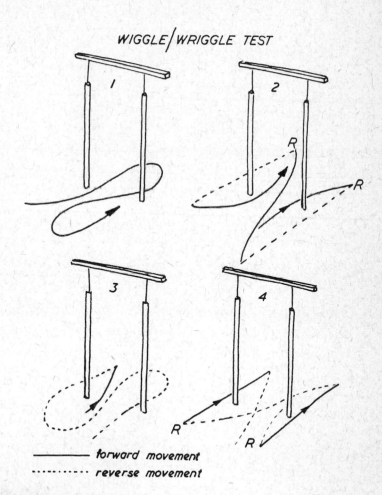

WIGGLE/WRIGGLE TEST

——————— forward movement
··············· reverse movement

and timing ceases when the bows leave the gate on the last move. The timekeeper and judge must stand in line with the poles. In competition no pole touching is permitted, any touch results in disqualification. In coaching work I find that a simple ten second penalty for each pole disturbed by boat, paddle or body added to elapsed time is a useful compromise.

In the wiggle competition one remains upright always; in the wriggle four rolls are introduced. A beginner should take about 200 seconds for a wiggle, an expert about 65 seconds. An expert doing the wriggle will take 65 to 70 seconds. An expert in top form will do the test in 60 to 62 seconds.

The moves are as follows, divided into four sequences. I first practise them using a pair of chairs and walking through the test.

Sequence one

    Forward through. Timing begins as bows enter gate.
    Right about turn.
    Forward through.
    Left about turn.
    Forward through.   Roll for wriggle.

Sequence two

    Reverse past gate on right.
    Forward through.   Roll for wriggle.
    Reverse past gate on left.
    Forward through.

Sequence three

    Reverse past gate on left again.
    Right about reverse turn.
    Reverse through gate.
    Left about reverse turn.
    Reverse through gate.   Roll for wriggle.

Sequence four

    Forward past gate on right.
    Reverse through gate.   Roll for wriggle.
    Forward past gate on left.
    Reverse through gate. Timing finishes.

Stunts

The seal launch is becoming much more popular since the advent of GRP canoes. Soft skinned and plywood canoes may be badly damaged in such a move. One sits in the canoe on the bankside, usually on a muddy shore or pebbly beach which is steeply pitched and, having adjusted spray deck and so on, slides forward into the water. In a turbulent crossing wave formation as off a promenade, a normal entry with the canoe alongside the promenade steps would place the canoeist in immediate danger of destructive banging against them. A seal launch down a sloping concrete groyne offers rapid penetration of the danger area and out into less dangerous waters say twenty feet away. The launch may be practised in the deep end of the baths by using a baths canoe which, because of its short length, is better for the purpose than a normal-length slalom canoe. One places the BAT at right angles to the bath edge with the forward edge of the seat just about over the

Court and Goodwin at Grantully Whit 1968. 'You paddle your end, and I'll paddle mine!'

edge of the bath. Take care in entering so as not to overbalance, adjust position and spray deck and, taking weight on knuckles on bath side, ease forward to the point of balance so that when leaning back the canoe will just not topple forward. Lean forward until the canoe slips off the edge, lean back at once and slide down into the water. Be ready with support strokes for either side. It is remarkably gentle and very like the real thing. The entry point may be made higher by using the various levels of the diving board (not above 5 ft.). The stunt may be varied by leaning forward on take off, but not off high places or one's face will receive a nasty impact from the water. The baths canoe, if it is especially small like the Water Baby, will loop forward on flat water if the bows are ballasted deep in the water. Looping may be done by diving with head forward from the baths side or by an assistant lifting one end of the canoe high above the water until the BAT is vertical.

Another stunt which has a useful function is changing places in deep water. Outdoors it should be practised in water about 12 in. deep, progressing to deeper water. In the baths it does not matter. The sequence of events is as follows:

1. Canoes face opposite ways, cockpits alongside each other.
2. Paddles behind backs, laid across the decks of the two canoes.
3. One canoeist sits up onto his paddle shaft almost centrally over the canoe but slightly toward the other canoe, so that the paddle shaft bears the weight between the canoes. (Don't sit in the middle or the shaft might break.)
4. The other does the same.
5. One puts his feet in the cockpit of the other canoe.
6. The other does the same.
7. Weight is transferred across the shaft to the opposite canoe.
8. One sits back firmly on the paddle shaft and steadies both canoes.
9. The other stands up, using partner's head as a 'bollard' to lean on.
10. He turns round and sits down in the other canoe.
11. He steadies both canoes whilst partner also stands and turns round.
12. Adjust position and spray decks and make comfortable.
13. Note that spray decks must fit each canoe equally well.

In practice this drill is useful on a sea trip when one of the group is cramped and must ease the ache in the legs or if one wishes to stand up in the canoe in order to take off extra clothing.

Finally it is useful to mention canoe polo. This can be played on any small area of water, such as a swimming-pool. Briefly the game is played five-a-side, seven minutes each way, usually in BATs, or similar baths boats. The goals are targets one metre square, suspended with the lower edge two metres above the water surface. The ball is a normal plastic basketball or a small football. The paddles are used *only* for propulsion. Efforts to use them to strike the ball may result in damage or, worse, injury. Players naturally wear helmets. The paddles are shorter than usual, with rounded plywood blades. Two teams lined up ready for the whistle, in team BATs, team shirts and helmets are an inspiring sight. Audience participation is enthusiastic and vociferous.

Canoe polo has developed and in 1972 has a national governing sub-commttiee of the British Canoe Union; rules have been made and limits to the size and shape of the canoes used have been stated. The BAT series which helped to develop an interest in this form of water sport has been found too small for top competition, and the largest canoe which satisfies the requirements is now a boat called the Vampire. As the designer of the BAT series I am now considering a new type, number eight in the BAT series, to be known as Dracula's Revenge. Competition certainly does quicken development, and canoeing has its sense of humour.

Chapter 21

Organising a Group

When taking groups of novices or canoeists with considerable experience afloat it becomes obvious that group organisation is very difficult. Asking people to keep to their allotted places and relying on them to do so is almost impossible. It may be that the sheer size of rivers and the sea allowing one the joyous freedom of wandering widely across the water, lost in a private world of escape from crowded roads, pavements, houses, shops and offices, is so attractive and persuasive that man-made rules come a poor second. Ratty in *Wind in the Willows* pinned it down exactly as the love of 'messing about in boats'.

With this primary difficulty in mind—that people afloat are difficult to organise for all manner of reasons, one must ask again the question, 'What will I say to the Coroner?' 'I didn't set out a form of organisation, sir, as it is well known that canoeists afloat are difficult to organise.' That would be a confession of incompetence difficult to surpass. Therefore, it is necessary to apply some form of order to a disorderly group. The following ideas have been moderately successful. Rivers and less confined waters each have their own requirements and are dealt with separately.

RIVER GROUP ORGANISATION

Size of group

The bigger the group, the more difficult it becomes to organise. There is a maximum number that any person can handle and an optimum number where the person in charge is so eased from the worry of responsibility that his service to the group in terms of interest and enthusiasm is much greater and the group derives great benefit from the experience.

In my experience Education Authorities assume that, if one is a

Devizes to Westminster long-distance canoe race, seventeen miles from start, at end of Bruce Tunnel, Savernake. These canoes are glass reinforced plastic K2s, not fast enough for sprinting, but good for this 24-hour-plus race.

teacher, groups of twenty or even more are quite possible, and some people have been known to be in charge of groups of fifty or more. Maximum and optimum numbers are set by the skill and experience of the person in charge and by the difficulty of the water on which one embarks as well as by the responsibility of the group as a whole.

Therefore, I would offer as a working rule that the optimum number for most situations is eight and the maximum number is twelve. I have taken groups of twenty when I have had a reliable person with me to help and the waters have been calm, and limited in extent. Moving groups are very different from static groups.

Preliminary organisation

It is very useful to reconnoitre the route in advance, either on foot or in the canoe with one or two skilled companions. Keep an eye open for local points of interest, obtain a book on the area and ask local people about local things.

From these surveys one can produce a duplicated sheet which can be handed out before the start and which people may look at and think about before they set out. Some forewarning of likely hazardous places is useful. The preliminary recce is useful to establish supply and access points, camp sites and so on. There may be strong opposition from fishing interests to be taken into account and perhaps permission to be obtained from estate offices before one wanders through the duck shooting grounds of some stately home.

The best advice I can give here is that one should ask the British Canoe Union for the advice of the local adviser on river access before setting off. The general secretary's address is 26-29 Park Crescent, London, W.1. If you know the river well you may be in a position to advise the BCU, and that advice would be welcome.

Group organisation

A novice group may produce the hard men who belt away into the distance, the potterers, the person unable to maintain a straight course, and so on. But they are all together at the beginning. Nominate a pathfinder, a person in charge and a pace setter who will sometimes be the pathfinder and sometimes not. The pathfinder should be someone who can read water, can find the way down a complex of shallows or rapids and who will wait and be available for rescuing others in difficulties. The pace setter must be someone with sufficient maturity to realise that some of the group are having difficulty staying with the pathfinder's pace. The person in charge should follow last and make it a rule that he passes no-one on the water except in an emergency. If someone should be unable to continue, he may detail off another to accompany the casualty on the banks.

The river imposes the limitations of its banks upon the group but it is possible temporarily to 'lose' large parts of the group in places where the river meanders through a sand and gravel working, through a complex of small islands or even down either side of an island in the river. One half of the group may want to tackle the easy straight rapid and the other may seek the excitement of a sudden weir drop round the other side of the island. Novice groups must all go by the same route.

Communication in the group is not easy. I find a powerful shout does most of what is necessary. It is a good idea to tell the group that if they hear a shout or a whistle signal, the leader should hold his paddle horizontally above his head, if the conditions permit. A paddle raised on end, the lower blade braced on the spray deck, is also a useful rallying signal and easier to support for some time than the quick rise and fall of a horizontal shaft in acknowledgement. Complicated whistle signals are fine if they can be understood but I find my shout has greater carrying power than a whistle.

If the leader is in difficulties, or sees difficulties ahead, all he need do is to stop and the rest of the group will catch up. The main difficulty lies not in stopping the group at the front, but in holding it back from the rear.

At the rear it is a good idea every now and then to count the canoeists on the water ahead. It should be done without fail after every obstacle or interference with the normal rate of progress.

Rapid negotiation

When approaching a rapid or other hazard the pathfinder will assess its difficulties and, if possible, attempt it. Once through he will wait below the obstacle until the group is all through. Remember to leave room for less experienced paddlers to break out of the stream; one should be close in below the obstacle whilst leaving enough room for the group to fit in.

Once the group is all through the person in charge checks that all is well and the group continues. Later, as confidence grows, it is quite reasonable for the pathfinder merely to slow down whilst watching the group through the obstacle and then to continue, without a prolonged halt. It is useful for the pathfinder to drift backwards down the river during this observation if conditions permit.

On continuous rough rapids, say Grade 3 and above, such step-by-step care in progress is not possible so the group must be self-reliant, rollers probably, in unladen canoes and in sub groups of three or four capable canoeists, each group independent of the others. In this case, the person in charge may not make contact with the whole group until the lunch-break or at the end of the day. A known rallying-place is essential. A land party is useful in maintaining overall contact.

There are many true stories of the police finding the remains of a smashed canoe and carrying out extensive and expensive dragging operations when a group which had lost a canoe in the rough had bundled the hapless paddler into the transport available without informing the police of the accident. One young man from London, camping and canoeing on the Eden in Cumberland, stepped ashore and pulled his canoe onto the bank but the water swept it away with all his camping equipment down river between impassable banks. So he went home to London, fed up. That was almost a Marie Celeste mystery for the police who later found the canoe drifting.

Finally, a plea for some identification on each canoe. It used to be the principle for all boats to have a name. Canoes seem not to be quite such revered objects as once they were. They are required only to do hard work successfully. The making of a GRP canoe may occupy about a day and a half and that does not make sufficient demands on the patience and perseverence of the maker for him to value it very much, except as a first class water vehicle. A name and address label resined to the inside of the hull beside the cockpit should be adequate.

SUMMARY

Preliminary organisation

BCU river advisory service.
Recce.
Permission to use water.
Permission to camp.
Access points.
Danger points.
Interesting points.
Rallying point. (Time and telephone number.)
Duplicated hand-out.

Launching organisation

Check canoes properly packed, rigged, identifiable.
Check canoeists properly dressed, lifejackets BSS 3595.
Inform group of command system.
Appoint pathfinder.
Appoint pace-setter/contact man.
Self in charge as 'sweeper-up', rescue and repair department.
Audible signals.
Visual signals.
Method at obstacles.
Count heads.

Moving organisation

Count heads every ten minutes.
Check lifejackets in use. BSS 3595.
Practise use of signals.
Practise ferry glides, break-in break-out, rapid negotiation.
Extra care at first obstacle.
Watch for drooping paddling action indicative of weariness.

Emergency organisation

Stop group. Deal with emergency. (In any order.)
Reorganise group. Salvage if possible. Repair.
If canoe lost INFORM POLICE.
Carry on if possible.

End of trip

Organise warm clothing for group.
Organise food for group.
Organise shelter for group.
Inform land party/base of arrival.
Necessary repairs ready for next day.
Talk about it.

SEA GROUP ORGANISATION

By sea canoeing I mean any canoeing on open waters which are
not closely limited by some natural obstacle or force, such as the
banks of a river or the shoreward surge of surf. I regard surfing

as having much more in common with rivers than with the sea,
from the canoeists point of view.

Sea canoeing quite definitely requires rescue skills in deep water.
The background knowledge required concerning weather and
waves is of great importance and one should not venture out onto
tidal water without some knowledge of the vast power of wave
forms in the air and the water.

Size of group

One should never go afloat with less than three, and more than
six can be difficult to handle. Therefore, smaller groups, each
self sufficient in rescue techniques, signalling power and emergency
resources, should be established. Whilst a person in charge
may have thirty or forty in his care, at least five or six trusted
deputies should be handling the other sub-groups with as
much, and perhaps more, authority than the river leader has.
If there is a really large group with six or seven sub-groups,
then there is a case for the person in charge to have no responsibility for individuals but to be free to wander among the groups
at will.

Personally, I would regard more than six as difficult on the sea
and eight as an absolute limit. Less than three there should not
be, more than six you are in a fix.

Preliminary organisation

This depends very much upon experience and careful thought.
One should be aware of the weather and this awareness is not
gained by a quick study the previous evening. Hammond Innes'
book *Atlantic Fury* is dramatic, very readable and most informa-
tive as to the behaviour of unstable air masses which whirl in
from the North Atlantic and whip up our seas. Telephone the
coastguard the preceding evening, and again just before launching,
for information on likely conditions, especially visibility, wind
velocity and direction, and air temperature. Apart from the
general conditions, a knowledge of cloud formations will alert
one to changes in air direction and temperature which may
herald rough seas locally even though the forecast may not
suggest it.

The coast should be *known*. I've been on a tide race at sea which almost frightened the wits out of me on a calm day with no wind and sunny skies. There was no way of seeing what would happen as that piece of sea is out of sight of the mainland behind an island two miles offshore; but I could have looked at a chart or asked a local.

Cliff faces, headlands and attendant overfalls, tide races, bay rips, local currents, all these and more may be anticipated. Some may be avoided by choosing a state of tide which is 'hanging' between ebb and flow, or by seeking a minimum rate of flow at half tide by choosing a time when neap tides are running. Some sea trip planning can and should be done many weeks ahead before booking the accommodation or the camp site. I prefer to set off and organise which route I take on arrival according to the prevailing conditions. A strong wind can easily ruin months of anticipation and planning. It took me five attempts and eight years before I actually crossed from the mainland to Inner Farne, off Northumberland, and that trip was perfect.

Ensure that sufficient signalling strength is carried. That can and should be done months ahead. It may take two months to obtain a firearms certificate for the miniflare.

Proper canoe and personal preparation must be made before the group assembles at the waterside. That has all been dealt with.

Just before launching telephone the coastguard and let him know what you are doing, where you are going and when you hope to arrive. Know the forecast weather and the coast. It has been known for watchers on the shore, not knowing of the self-rescue capabilities of a skilled group, to call out the helicopter and lifeboat to what appeared to be a really nasty off-shore reef accident. One was hurled into the water, another did a double backward loop over him and a third just made it out. Twenty minutes later and 200 yards away the whole group re-assembled rescue complete, had a breather, said 'What-ho!' or words to that effect and set off home, waving to the passing lifeboat and 'chopper'.

Another couple, having fun in rough waters off Hartlepool, found the lifeboat alongside. 'All right lads, you're OK now, we've got you' shouted the lifeboat man. When the canoeists declined the offer the comment from the lifeboat was, 'We are double blowed if we are coming out on a Sunday afternoon for a non-rescue, so ***** climb aboard!' Being diplomatic, and realising that it is sometimes better to receive than to give, they climbed aboard.

Inform the coastguard service that you have flares and that you will use them if necessary. In all my time on the sea, only twice have I considered it might be necessary to let off my flares though, in fact, I did not.

After landing inform the coastguard and your base that you have done so. A good plan is to have someone, somewhere, maybe hundreds of miles away, on the telephone and ready to call for help if you have not checked in within, say, three hours of the ETA. Such a 'long-stop' should be informed of any change of plan before setting off, otherwise an emergency search may set off on the wrong foot.

Estuaries impose their own difficulties in terms of shipping channels, buoyage, mud flats, sand bars and surf in the mid-estuary areas, and so on. Estuaries are perhaps even more demanding in terms of local knowledge than the open sea. Access by road in emergency is often impossible. One must know of these difficulties.

Group organisation

The group is not bound by banks close alongside to trail along Indian file. They may, and do, spread out both lengthways and sideways all over the sea. This is not too bad provided the wave height is less than eye level, say two feet six inches, but above this one quite suddenly loses visual contact with anyone more than a wavelength away. In choppy waters this can be within a very few yards.

Wind and sun direction are important. The leader should be upwind and down-sun from his group if the group is to hear what is said and see what signals are given. This, of course, puts the leader (who is the person in charge) at a disadvantage but skill and knowledge should overcome that. A roughly triangular formation with the leader to the rear, the sun over the group-side shoulder and the wind over the offside shoulder is a good place to be. The group should maintain about two canoe-lengths between each pair, sideways and endways, for wake eddies do pull canoes together and it is ludicrous to see two paddlers repeatedly barging into each other with miles of sea to play with. In any event the group should not spread beyond audible contact

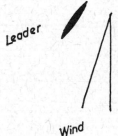

Group positioning

one with another.

Group organisation is fairly simple and regular pauses to see one another through obstacles are not necessary. However, a much greater responsibility comes upon the leader in seeking out helping currents and eddies around cliff faces and reefs, and in coming ashore at the least troublesome spot. Of course, it may be a group of the hard boys in which case evidence of thrashing surf is sought with joy.

Remember that surfing beaches are often suitable for swimmers so one should come ashore before starting continuous surfing to check where the swimmers are. Popular beaches will have regular lifeguards and they will possibly have staked out a surfing area for canoes and boards and you will be directed to these areas.

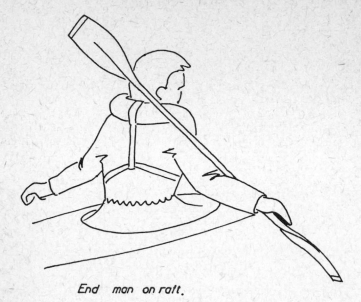

End man on raft.

If, whilst out at sea, the group has an emergency it is likely to be one of several. Capsizes in rough sea usually mean that if one member of the group cannot cope, others are likely not to. It is then necessary to pull the group together immediately into a raft which is manoeuvred by the end men using their paddles single handed across the back of the neck. Once the raft is established auto-suggested capsizes are prevented, one's group risk is lessened and rescue may proceed. However, the person in the water will act like a sea anchor for the rescue, the raft will tend to drift downwind and a good deal of sea-room appears between rescuer and raft very quickly. The use of the raft depends on how quickly the rescue may be done and how much leeway one has before the raft drifts into danger itself. In this case it is necessary to have a raft leader who takes the place of the river pathfinder, and the person in charge becomes the rescuer. The raft leader must have the ability to decide what to do, even to abandon temporarily the two or three in the rescue if this appears necessary. It may be that the person in charge will have to lead the others to safety leaving a rescuer selected from the group to handle the person in the water.

CHECK LIST

Preliminary organisation

Admiralty chart.
Reed's Almanak.
Local tide charts.
Canoeing in Britain guide to surfing beaches.
Flares and firearms certificates obtained.
Access: Launching.
　　　　Along route.
　　　　Landing place.
Know: Weather.
　　　Waves.
　　　Tides.
　　　Currents.
　　　GPO weather report previous night.
Base informed.
Coastguard/police informed.
Issue duplicated handout in good time for group to learn route.

Launching organisation

Check: Weather, wind, etc.
　　　　Sun direction and sun glasses.
　　　　Flares and signals available.
　　　　Emergency food and clothing.
　　　　Canoes properly packed and rigged.
　　　　Canoeists properly clothed and lifejackets BSS 3595 worn.
　　　　Everyone knows route and plan.
　　　　Base.
　　　　Coastguard.
　　　　Shore party, transport.
Select: Groups.
　　　　Raft leaders.
Count heads.

Moving organisation

Count heads every ten minutes.
Practise: Signals (but *not* flares).

Rafting.
Deep water rescue (if there is time).
Check position relative to group and direction of movement.
Watch: Clouds.
Land.
Time.
Watch out for: Sagging paddle strokes and evidence of fatigue.
Early signs of exposure.
Escape routes and landing places.
Ships, buoys, reefs, etc.
BE AWARE.

End of trip

Inform: Shore party, transport.
Coastguard.
Base.
Organise: Warm clothing.
Warm food.
Shelter.
Load canoes.
Return to base.
Talk about it.

INDEX